CONCEPT MARKETING
FOR COMMUNITIES

CONCEPT MARKETING
FOR COMMUNITIES

CAPITALIZING ON UNDERUTILIZED RESOURCES
TO GENERATE GROWTH AND DEVELOPMENT

RHONDA PHILLIPS

Westport, Connecticut
London

Library of Congress Cataloging-in-Publication Data

Phillips, Rhonda.
    Concept marketing for communities : capitalizing on underutilized resources to
generate growth and development / Rhonda Phillips.
        p.   cm.
    Includes bibliographical references and index.
    ISBN 0–275–96798–0 (alk. paper)
    1. Community development.   2. Place marketing.   I. Title.
HN49.C6P46   2002
307.1′4—dc21   2001054569

British Library Cataloguing in Publication Data is available.

Library of Congress Catalog Card Number: 2001054569
ISBN: 0–275–96798–0

First published in 2002

Praeger Publishers, 88 Post Road West, Westport, CT 06881
An imprint of Greenwood Publishing Group, Inc.
www.praeger.com

Printed in the United States of America

The paper used in this book complies with the
Permanent Paper Standard issued by the National
Information Standards Organization (Z39.48–1984).

10 9 8 7 6 5 4 3 2 1

Copyright Acknowledgments

Photograph 5.1 and 5.2: For additional information and a free Cape May Visitor's Guide, please
contact the Chamber of Commerce of Greater Cape May at (609) 884–5508 or online at
www.capemaychamber.com

Adventure is the vitaminizing element in histories both individual and social.

William Bolitho
Twelve Against the Gods: Introduction

෴

This book is dedicated to the memory of my father, and first teacher,
Kenneth Wayne Phillips, 1930–1991.
His adventurous spirit and willingness to seek beyond the ordinary
inspired the idea for this book, as well as many other journeys.

Contents

Illustrations

Preface

Episodic memories are those triggered by an encounter that brings to mind past occurrences. Whenever I encounter information about a community that is engaging in concept marketing, it triggers the following episodic memory:

It was a warm spring day in 1970, and I asked my father, again, where we were. Sampling cheese in a shop that could have easily blended in on the streets of Amsterdam, I was dazed, and delighted, by what I was seeing. We were in Holland, Michigan. I clutched my bag, containing a miniature pair of wooden shoes, and waited for him to explain, again, why this town did not look like anything I had ever seen before.

Enthralled by the uniqueness of something different, at eight years of age, I was experiencing my first taste of community concept marketing, in the surrealistic fashion.

The fascination with seeking out "something different" in communities never ended, and through the years, the unusual, the surreal, the re-creations were sought out. Questions were formulated through the years that led to this research: Why are some communities able to create that "something different" that attracts so many? How do they accomplish it? Why are some communities successful and others not? And perhaps most importantly how can those communities that desperately need revitalization learn from others, so they can experience the benefits of community economic development as well?

They do exist, and serve as a treasured find, these communities that are something different. This book is a tribute to these communities and serves to provide insight into the process of creating revitalization through innovative approaches. The idea for *Concept Marketing for Communities* is a culmination of years of research, visiting and working with communities, and investigating what parameters determine community economic success. The focus of the research is on how small and mid-sized communities are able to overcome obstacles of economic re-structuring and other global forces that have crippled the economies of many cities and towns throughout the United States. The intended audiences for this book are community economic development and planning educators and researchers; students of urban and regional planning, community economic development, tourism, and public administration; community economic development professionals; and civic leaders interested in devising concept marketing approaches.

Acknowledgments

There are several persons who deserve special recognition: as always, Jay and the rest of my family for their encouragement; Jennifer Moreau, for her capable assistance and unparalleled organizational skills; Maury Forman of the Washington State Department of Commerce, Trade, and Economic Development and Edward Blakely of the New School for Social Research for their thoughtful comments; my colleagues at the University of Florida and the University of Southern Mississippi; Bill Sheppard of the John C. Stennis NASA Space Center; and Sandra Taylor Danes for her unwavering support.

The author would like to thank all those who participated in the national survey to identify innovative communities, including state departments of economic development, and especially the following persons:

Elizabeth Bailey, Curator, Mid-Atlantic Center for the Arts, Cape May, New Jersey
Delanie Bartlette, Publications Director, Eureka Springs Chamber of Commerce, Eureka Springs, Arkansas
Nikki Beare, Beare's Books 'N Things & Historical Bookshelf, Havana, Florida
Edna Brooks Pittman, Community Development Department, City of Toppenish, Washington
Jackie Burgett, Mountain View Chamber of Commerce
Adam Cermak, Director, Madison County Chamber of Commerce, Winterset, Iowa
Fred Constantino, Land Management Specialist, Hudson County Economic Development Corporation, Secaucus, New Jersey
Sandy Forstner, Austin Chamber of Commerce, Austin, Minnesota
Karen Garner, Economic Development Analyst, City of Roseville, California
Bernard Groff, Administrative Director, Cape May County, Cape May, New Jersey
Iris Harper, Executive Director, Natchitoches Parish Tourist Commission, Natchitoches, Louisiana
Mary Harris, Hormel Foods, Austin, Minnesota

Keith Henderson, Owner, H&H Antiques, Havana, Florida
Vicky Heitman, Director, Loveland Chamber of Commerce, Loveland, Colorado
Dusty Huckabee, Roswell, New Mexico
Dean Jacobs, Executive Director, Valentine Chamber of Commerce, Valentine,
    Nebraska
Joe Kammlah, Fredericksburg Chamber of Commerce, Fredericksburg, Texas
Roberta Kerby, Toppenish Chamber of Commerce, Toppenish, Washington
Lee Krohn, Town Planner, Manchester, Vermont
Sally Hallan Laukitis, Executive Director, Holland Area Convention & Visitors
    Bureau, Holland, Michigan
Wanda Maltbie, Boaz Chamber of Commerce, Boaz, Alabama
Robert McBride, Director, RAMP, Bellows Falls, Vermont
Mary Ann McCall, Art and Advertising Director, Alpine Helen/White County
    Convention & Visitors Bureau, Helen, Georgia
Sue McManus, Executive Director, Downtown Business Association, Vacaville,
    California
Judy Moen, Cle Elum/Roslyn Chamber of Commerce, Roslyn, Washington
Rita Morgan, Coordinator, Alpine Helen/White County Convention & Visitors
    Bureau, Helen, Georgia
Kim Patterson, Director of Publicity and Special Events, Chamber of Commerce of
    Greater Cape May, Cape May, New Jersey
Riddle, Marcy, Boaz Chamber of Commerce Board of Directors, Boaz, Alabama
Ginny Moody, Mayors Office, City of Eunice, Louisiana
Gary Noble, Branson/Lakes Area Chamber of Commerce, Branson, Missouri
Mike Palombo, Economic Development Manager, City of Vacaville, California
Jennifer Pearce, Director of Public Relations, The Longaberger Company, Newark,
    Ohio
Eldon Ranney, Antiques dealer, Walnut, Iowa
Dan Rovero, Mayor, City of Putnam, Connecticut
Cindy Samuels, Spamtown USA Festival Director, Austin, Minnesota
Elda Schiesser, Author, *The Swiss Endure, Year-by-Year: A Chronological History,
    1845–1995*, New Glarus, Wisconsin
Irene Seel, Executive Assistant to the Director, Greater San Antonio Area Tourism
    Council, San Antonio, Texas
Jane Shipman, Chairman, Arkansas Folk Festival, Mountain View, Arkansas
Leslie Thompson, Roswell, New Mexico
Dina Wagner, Harrisburg Regional Chamber of Commerce, Harrisburg, Pennsylvania
Barbara Walden, City Clerk and Treasurer, City of Boaz, Alabama
Charlie Walker, Director of Economic Development, Roswell Chamber of
    Commerce, Roswell, New Mexico
Diane Weiland, Director of Tourism, Cape May County, Cape May, New Jersey
Craig Willis, Director, Mount Dora Chamber of Commerce, Mount Dora, Florida
Martin Teller, Principal Planner, Cape May County Planning Commission, Cape May,
    New Jersey
Jackie Traylor, Executive Director, Solvang Danish Village Conference and Visitors
    Bureau, Solvang, California
Michael Zuckerman, Director, Mid-Atlantic Center for the Arts, Cape May, New
    Jersey

1

Introduction

"There isn't any there there," Gertrude Stein was credited with saying after visiting an American city. In many instances, this short quote could be applied to numerous towns and cities across the United States. There are, mercifully, exceptions. The communities presented in this book are exceptions, and *exceptional*, possessing a definitive sense of place. They have managed to create, or re-create, a style, ambience, or character that transcends the ordinary and can be used as the basis for community economic development, and in some cases, survival as a community. There *is* something there, in these communities.

Cities and towns are using innovative approaches to encourage growth and development of their communities with increasing frequency and zeal. An approach sweeping through many communities is the idea of *concept marketing*—that is, finding a niche or specialty to create "brand" recognition for a community. In these instances, the brand is some unique aspect of a community that serves as a basis for garnering external investment, tourism, and other revenue-generating activities. Community concept marketing is an intentional, goal-driven effort to build a community's identity to the external environment. It capitalizes on underutilized resources to generate growth and development. Sometimes these resources are inherent within the community; other times, they literally have to be created.

This trend transcends efforts to build tourism—it incorporates overall community economic development approaches, including integrating with planning and other activities at the local level. Communities are reinventing themselves to prosper and are doing so in innovative and creative approaches that go beyond the ordinary. The impetus for this book grew from observations of, and work with, communities throughout the United States that are concerned with the future growth and direction of their towns and cities. It became apparent that some communities stand above the rest in their efforts to create something unique and effective. For the most part, these communities are small to mid-sized, in terms of population, but "giants" in the way they approach community economic development. With refreshing creativity and zeal matched by few other entities, these communities have devised innovative ways to market themselves and capture economic development benefits for their citizens. This book presents these innovators.

Ranging from small towns with populations less than 500, to the largest at 84,000 citizens, these communities utilize a variety of approaches to build their concepts. More than just seeking publicity, or adoption of a particular architectural style, concept marketing incorporates the whole community development framework, from design to planning standards, to seeking out viable public-private collaborations. While the approaches to concept marketing vary as much as individual communities, there are a few common approaches, or concept categories, that have emerged. These are summarized in the following five categories.

Popular Culture. Some towns embrace an aspect of popular culture as a platform for devising their marketing approach. This includes using art, music, and filmmaking as a method to construct a concept. Entertainment is a key element, whether the production or performance of it.

Corporate Culture. Several communities link to a corporate identity and use the larger recognition of the corporation as a base to build upon. This approach—corporate iconicism—can literally brand a community.

Retail. Appealing to the enthusiastic shopper, some communities build their concepts around shopping opportunities. The venue may be offered in conjunction with revitalization of a historic downtown district, it might focus on themed shopping, such as antiquing, or it can concentrate on outlet shopping.

Tradition. Heritage and cultural aspects of a community are increasingly utilized to serve as the foundation for developing marketing concepts. This marketing approach focuses on applications using historic preservation and ethnicity.

Surrealistic. This category runs the gamut from creating the atmosphere of the completely surreal to recapturing the historical ambience of a community. Concept marketing approaches based on surrealism require boldness and a high level of creativity and generally go beyond what is normally anticipated in a community economic development effort.

CONTEXT OF COMMUNITY ECONOMIC DEVELOPMENT (CED)

Why are communities concerned with concept marketing at all? Marketing is generally considered the purview of the private sector—selling products and services to consumers, often through expensive advertising campaigns. Is it not enough to function as a community, with local government providing services funded through taxes and other sources of revenues? If communities are functioning effectively, is there a reason to "market" them?

In order to understand why cities and towns embark on marketing efforts, as would a private corporation, it is important to understand the nature of community economic development. Because concept marketing, as applied in this book, reflects a broad development approach, it is necessary to understand the context of community economic development.

From the public sector perspective, communities generally have two major approaches to encouraging growth and development at their disposal:

1. Investing directly in supporting infrastructures, such as transportation improvements, public buildings, and public space (parks and recreational facilities)
2. Public control over private investments via land use and other regulatory controls (Levy 1997).

The first approach requires investment of funds, either from revenues or through debt financing. The second approach entails instatement of regulatory measures such as a comprehensive land use plan with zoning, design standards, historic district designation, or conservation lands. Local governments can also provide funding to nonprofit groups, such as a chamber of commerce or convention and visitors bureau, to provide marketing services. This is usually arranged on a service contract basis. Of course, there are many variations. For example, some communities operate departments of economic development and planning to directly interface with prospective investors. Basically, there are three sectors involved in community economic development activities: (1) private sector—utility companies and banks; (2) public sector—either directly or indirectly at the federal, state, and local levels; and (3) nonprofit sector—organizations representing citizens, other organizations, the public sector, and/or private business concerns.

Another factor that influences how economic development is approached in a community is the orientation of the community towards growth. Is it a growth-controlled environment, with development tightly regulated? Is it growth accommodating, with few regulatory measures in place, seeking new investments and developments? Or is it growth managing, seeking a balance between development and the goals of the community? Whatever the orientation, most cities and towns include in their definition of community economic development some phrase about maintaining or improving quality of life. The most commonly encountered definition of economic development is that stated by the American Economic Development Council: "Economic development: The process of creating wealth through the mobilization of human, financial, capital, physical and natural resources to generate marketable goods and services" (American Economic Development Council 1984:18).

With an emphasis on "marketable goods and services," the definition is not inclusive of the community's needs and goals and does not really include an explicit statement about quality of life considerations. "Economic development" is a loaded term, with varying conceptions, definitions, theories, and politicians driving it. While definitions obviously vary depending on the community's orientation towards development, a slightly better one is: Community economic development: activities undertaken for the purposes of increasing standards of living through generation of greater per capita income, increased quality and quantity of employment opportunities, and improved quality of life for the persons represented within the development district. This definition shifts the focus from counting the number of jobs created in a community as a result of economic development efforts to include other measurement variables, both qualitative and quantitative. This is preferable, since ideally, economic development should be judged in terms of effects on the community, not just in quantitative terms. Development should be goal-oriented change, not change for the sake of change. Including the concept of "community" in the term broadens its scope by incorporating the following underlying premise: Community economic development is based on the belief that citizens have the capability and responsibility to undertake community-directed initiatives for the good of all its members.

Community economic development can be a powerful force and typically begins when individuals believe they can make a contribution to maintaining or improving the quality of life in their community. A crucial component is belief—a potent force that can raise collective power and lead to action and results. Although communities can change on the basis of one person's actions, community economic development is best performed as a group activity, with strategies emerging from the decision of a group of people to take action. It requires community-wide initiatives, which in turn requires collaboration. Another way of thinking about community economic development is to think of it as community building.

Typically, economic development approaches generally include the following three activities: (1) industrial and commercial *recruitment* of outside interests to locate within the community; (2) *retention and expansion* of existing local employers; and (3) promoting entrepreneurial growth, or *small business development*. Community economic development broadens the range to include not only these traditional activities but also any or all of the following elements:

1. Stabilize economic conditions through public sector investments and coordination with private and nonprofit development organizations.

2. Increase quality and quantity of housing to support development and improve quality of life.

3. Improve commercial functions of the community via supporting zoning, infrastructure investments, and programmatic elements, such as business improvement districts or tax increment financing districts.

4. Improve the physical aspects of the community via land use planning for traffic flow; public space including recreation and parking facilities; and incorporating multimodal transportation facilities.

5. Integrate concepts of urban design, such as design review and standards to facilitate the physical attractiveness of the community.

6. Provide a variety of public services to support quality development outcomes, such as a high quality educational system and business support services (e.g., permitting processing, etc.).

The context of community economic development is thus inclusive and broad in focus: it literally endeavors to affect the entire realm of communities. Quality of life becomes a goal in itself, and the approaches taken are influenced by what citizens want to achieve in their communities.

Brief Review of the Theoretical Basis of CED

Alfred Hirschman in his classic work, *The Strategy of Economic Development*, proposed that economic development "depends not so much on finding optimal combination for given resources and factors of production as on calling forth and enlisting for development purposes resources and abilities that are hidden, scattered or badly utilized" (Hirschman 1958:5). It is unlikely that Hirschman envisioned his definition of economic development being applied in the context of concept marketing, yet it is a very appropriate description of its goal: capitalizing on underutilized resources to generate growth and development, and hence the subtitle for this book.

Most theory that focuses on economic development infrequently touches on theory as applied to the community level. There does exist, however, a vast array of theories designed to explain social and economic development—most are distinguished by their level of analysis. Jaffee (1998:9) lists the common levels as: international (world economic institutions and interactions); societal (national level political, economic and social institutions and policies); organizational (structure and management of business enterprises); and individual (values, attitudes, motives, and characteristics). None of these sufficiently explain community level economic development.

As Blakely (1994:53) explains, the sum of theories of growth and development may be expressed as: Local/Regional Development = f(natural resources, labor, capital investment, entrepreneurship, transport, communication, industrial composition, technology, size, export market, international economic situation, local government capacity, national and state government spending, and development supports). However, weights are not given to the various factors and the practitioner is provided with little guidance in local community economic development decision making.

Despite the paucity of explicitly stated theory for community level economic development, it is important to pursue its investigation. Theories provide an analytic framework for understanding phenomena. Because theory can be descriptive or predictive in nature, it helps to simplify complex processes. In other words, theory serves as a basis for understanding what is observed and experienced and thereby motivates actions (Malizia and Feser 1999). There are actually theories that hold relevance for community economic development, although the general premise of these theories was not necessarily based on that level of analysis originally. Theories of development from economics, business administration, public administration, regional science, urban and regional planning, and even psychology can provide insight into community economic development (Bingham and

Mier 1993). Commonly encountered theories for economic development include sector theory, location theory, growth pole theory, regional concentration/agglomeration and diffusion theory, theories of entrepreneurship, neoclassical growth theory, interregional trade theory, and product cycle theory (Bingham and Mier 1993; Malizia and Feser 1999). Deficiencies are found in each type; for example, the linkages between economic base, income inequality, and growth trajectories are especially lacking (Howland 1993:76). While none have emerged yet with a high level of explanatory and predictive powers when applied to community economic development, it is vital to keep exploring theory so that insight can be gained.

In *Theories of Local Economic Development* (Bingham and Mier 1993), over fifty theories from various disciplines that relate to economic development were analyzed. A synthetic theory of local economic development could not be articulated, given the complexity and number of related theories; instead, the authors promoted the use of generative metaphors to investigate the many facets of development. Metaphors can be used to construct "stories" of local economic development, with "metaphors providing the inspirational spine to the stories and thus a framework for incorporating the diverse theories of development into practical application" (Bingham and Mier 1993:xvi). Concept marketing provides a basis for development stories.

Economic base theory is probably the most widely recognized theory within community economic development. Essentially, the theory states that demand emanating from outside a region (or community) for that area's products or services is the primary determinant of economic outcomes (Malizia and Feser 1999). These products and services sold to external entities are called basic industries; those that are consumed by local citizens are termed nonbasic industries. Economic base theory has been used to predict the future growth of an area, as well as identify target industries to recruit into the community. It holds particular relevance for concept marketing because many of the approaches rely on creating basic industries in the form of tourism or attracting shoppers from beyond the community to retail enterprises.

One justification used to plan for and invest in community economic development is found in the idea of market failure. This idea actually is used explicitly or implicitly (as is often the case) as justification for marketing a community for purposes of economic development. The perfect market economy model "assumes perfect communication between market participants, no externalities, a very large number of standardized items or units for sale, and a large enough number of buyers and sellers such that no participant can distort the market" (Lyons and Hamlin 2001:xii). Too many distortions and imperfections exist to achieve these conditions; hence, the concept of market failure. Therefore, local government and organizations involved in community economic development justify their actions as helping the market to be more efficient and equitable. This is one of the most frequently applied economic concepts to the practice of local community economic development. It also is relevant for concept marketing because many communities are too small or isolated to be "on the radar screen." Thus, marketing helps to overcome the problem of a lack of information about the communities—a problem attributed to market failure.

COMMUNITY MARKETING APPROACHES

Marketing of cities and towns has existed in one form or another for centuries. Competing with other communities for resources, economic activities, and even residents is readily observed: most cities have some version of "marketing" activities, whether explicit or implicit in nature. Further, cities operate within markets, with the operation of these markets influencing the markets of other communities (Gold and Ward 1994). Attempting to influence the outcomes of these markets, intervention in the form of marketing is utilized.

Place Marketing

Marketing for cities, towns, and regions is somewhat different from marketing in the private business sector. While the focus in the private sector is on the selling of products and services to consumers, the focus for marketing geographic entities is broader. "Place marketing" is defined as a "process whereby local activities are related as closely as possible to the demands of the targeted customer . . . (with the intention) to maximize the efficient social and economic functioning of the area concerned, in accordance with whatever wider goals have been established" (Gold and Ward 1994:41).

The practice of place promotion encompasses myriad approaches that public, private, and nonprofit (otherwise known as nongovernmental organizations) entities utilize to sell the image of communities (Philo and Kearns 1993:1). Marketing as an activity of the public sector has become an accepted, and even expected, phenomenon. In fiscal year 1998–1999, the state tourism offices in the United States spent $524 million on promotional marketing, up nearly 8 percent from the year before (Schmidt 1999). Communities and states are advised to think strategically about market planning, in order to respond to the challenges of intensifying competition (Kotler, Haider, and Rein 1994; Nykiel and Jascolt 1998).

A sort of "competitive ethos of selling places" has emerged, requiring the public sector to participate (Ward 1998:5). Actions by the public sector, from service provision to infrastructure investments, impact the place-selling ethos (Ward 1998:3), and the political environment of the community. Since politics is essentially about control, the public sector with its influence on policy, becomes a major participant or player in the creation and marketing of places (Ashworth and Voogd 1990; Hall and Jenkins 1995; Hall 1994; Kearns and Philo 1993). It is an usual combination in some aspects; place marketing is an aspect of public or quasipublic policy and should embody ideas such as public good and benefit without harming other communities (Gold and Ward 1994:7). Yet, the nature of place marketing is competitive. This situation leads to interesting public policy and politics.

Private Sector Marketing Applied to Community Development

Some of the principles of private sector marketing can be applied to marketing of communities. Marketing has evolved to include wide applicability of some of its principles; increasingly these principles are utilized by public and nonprofit sector organizations (Heath and Wall 1992:6). This lesson is clearly seen in the evolution of Nantucket, Massachusetts. Walter Beinecke first visited Nantucket in 1923. During the 1960s, with the economy of Nantucket stagnant, Beinecke and partners, Sherburne Associates, decided to redevelop their holdings (several hotels, residences, and over forty commercial sites) as a resort destination. Using $10 million of borrowed funds, they renovated the historic properties into upscale space, attracting artisan galleries, restaurants, and other uses. "We thought that the island's proximity to Boston and New York, especially in regards to the time to sail from there to here, made it an ideal resort destination," explained Beinecke (Beinecke 2001). Two driving elements focused the developers' attention: distinction and quality. The distinction was clear for Nantucket: a long and rich history as the former whaling capital of North America, and 1,300 buildings over 100 years old in relatively good condition. The quality component was built into the process from the beginning, using the retail concept of trading up. The developers decided to operate on the premise that visitors would pay extra for quality coupled with distinction.

Beinecke developed the following formula to build the resort concept:

$$V \text{ ✻ } AT = \pm \, GI$$

where V is the number of visitors, AT is the average transactions by the visitors, and GI is the gross income (Beinecke 2001:1). Depending on the average transactions, the gross income fluctuates. "I learned early on that the key is to increase the expenditures by the visitor, and the way to do this is through offering the best quality services and products," Beinecke elaborated. Another concept applied is to limit the supply, so that the number of visitors is not overwhelming. When the developers started the resort development process, Nantucket had a population of less than 2,000; in the 1970s population was 3,500; in the early 1990s, 6,500; and is estimated at 9,500 in 2001. An estimated 55,000 tourists visit Nantucket during the summer, swelling the population tremendously. Supply has been limited by placing over 40 percent of Nantucket's land into conservation space, with acquisition funds generated via a 2 percent surcharge on all real estate transactions on the island. Land use regulations and other planning measures put into place over the last decade have further controlled and guided development. The quality component continues to be controlled via the land use and design regulations. For example, Nantucket has no fast food restaurant chains, traffic lights, or neon signs. Independently operated shops, galleries, and restaurants offer the visitor a unique experience.

The formula can be applied in concept marketing approaches. By offering a combination of quality and distinction, concept marketing communities can achieve development goals. However, even with much success as measured by an increase in visitors and visitor expenditures, communities are finding that growth confers problems as well. The ability to keep up with infrastructure demands, preserve the community character and culture, provide enough services to visitors and citizens, and deal with traffic congestion and lack of affordable housing are all issues that growing communities must face. These are the areas in which the public sector must collaborate with the private and nonprofit sectors to identify community goals and develop a comprehensive plan on how to achieve them. Land use and other regulatory mechanisms must be put into place to guide growth and achieve desired outcomes, rather than waiting for issues to reach crisis status. Too often communities invoke the use of community planning as a reaction to negative outcomes of uncontrolled growth when they should have already had in place a system to prevent crises. Community concept marketing approaches should be based on a fully integrated development method, utilizing the tools of land use planning, community participation, and other techniques to achieve the best possible and desired outcomes.

Theming

A pervasive change in the nature of marketing has occurred. This applies to both private and public sector marketing efforts. Since World War II, the focus has shifted from sales highlighting the value of the product or service to marketing symbolic values. Market segmentation has increased to the point that in order to appeal to a highly differentiated consumer public, theming is used as a direct marketing approach (Gottdiener 1997). It is also speculated that the change is due to the increasingly hedonistic nature of consumers who continually seek to be entertained (Wolf 1999). Consumers are seeking "utopias of consumption" for fulfilling simultaneously entertainment, service, and shopping needs (Crawford 1992). Communities are responding by creating an aura of utopian alternatives to everyday life. "The city as theme park" is becoming more commonplace (Sorkin 1992), with all its outcomes, both positive and negative. "It's as if our theme parks have o'erleapt the gates and run amuck. Everything now strives to look like something else, to evoke a distant place or era" (Curtis 2000:35). Consumers seemingly have grown to expect themed marketing approaches, both in their commercial encounters and in the greater context of communities.

What is the concept of theming as applied to communities? Essentially it implies that an environment is created, one in which the ordinary is left behind and the extraordinary is the standard. Many dismiss the phenomenon as an overzealous market response, while others view it as an opportunity for declining communities to revitalize. Some have attacked the concept as destroying public space (Gottdiener 1997; Sorkin 1992), yet many communities have applied theming concepts in conjunction with creating *more* public space. The relationship between public space and concept marketing is explored in the following section.

Desire for the Public Realm

One explanation why community concept marketing is successful in the United States can be found in James Howard Kunstler's answer to the question: Why is Disney World such a success? In *Home From Nowhere*, he presents the following information in response to this question:

> Americans love Disney World back home because the everyday places where they live and go about their business are so dismal that Disney World seems splendid in comparison. American cities are dismal. The majority of American small towns have become dismal. . . . The design quality of Disney World in Orlando . . . is about 1.5 notches better than the average American suburban shopping mall or housing subdivision—so Americans love it. (Kunstler 1996:36–37)

He further explains that what is missing in most American cities, towns, and suburbs is the public realm. It is defined as "that portion of our everyday world which belongs to everybody and to which everybody ought to have equal access most of the time" (Kunstler 1996:36). The public realm in the United States has been destroyed or has deteriorated, so when Disney World provides a substitute for it, Americans respond favorably, even if they are not aware of the concept of public realm.

Community concept marketing approaches literally seek to provide a strong sense of place and invariably incorporate some element of the public realm into redevelopment efforts. Perhaps this is one of the major reasons that concept marketing approaches, when appropriately applied, can help reinvigorate communities. Many of the concept marketing communities described in this book aggressively plan for and implement public space in their development plans. Parks and other public spaces are the norm for these communities, rather than the exception.

METHODOLOGY

Cities and towns using concept marketing approaches are widely dispersed throughout the United States. Several methods were used to identify innovative communities to profile in this book. The first method was to search through the literature of major academic databases and relevant trade publications and to engage directly with communities. Second, a mail survey was sent to all fifty state-level economic and community development agencies in the United States. The survey asked the agency to list community locations and contacts of those they considered innovative in several categories, according to definitions provided in the survey instrument. This process was supplemented by selective contact with community and economic development practitioners for their input and advice in identifying innovative concept marketing approaches.

The third phase was to conduct a telephone interview with community-level contacts to discern the level of marketing efforts and the intensity of the approach utilized. Over 200 communities were identified as part of this research;

information from many of these communities has been integrated into the information presented within this book. A core group of 60 communities were then selected for in-depth research of their marketing efforts. This group was further reduced to 28 "profile" communities, and the vignettes for each of these are presented in the following five chapters. These communities exemplify the variety and creativity inherent in concept marketing applications for achieving positive growth and change. While the applications vary widely, there are some commonalities among the communities—thus, they have been categorized according to their concept approach.

Another shared characteristic of the profile communities is that of population size. All are considered small to mid-sized, with populations ranging from 84,000 in Vacaville, California, to 300 in the village of Helen, Georgia. Table 1.1 lists the profile communities presented in this book.

The communities profiled in this book were selected from a diverse array of contexts and geographical settings. Figure 1.1 maps their locations.

OVERVIEW AND STRUCTURE

The structure of this book is to provide analysis of each major category of concept marketing approaches in the following four chapters. The categories are: popular and corporate culture (music, filmmaking, art, corporate iconicity); retail (outlets and themes, including antiquing); tradition (historic preservation and ethnicity); and surrealism (creating unprecedented concepts). The format is to introduce the general category, followed by the community vignettes. Each vignette provides a summary of the community's

- overview and historical context,
- impetus for change, or the reason the concept idea was selected,
- process used to develop the concept, and
- outcomes of the community concept marketing approach.

Each chapter concludes with a summary of the approach. Chapter 7 concludes with implications and assessments for analyzing the applicability of community concept development, as well as ideas for implementation.

The material presented illustrates the bases for building community marketing and development approaches. Communities that use popular culture applications are described in Chapter 2. In some communities, popular and corporate culture provides the marketing niche on which to build promotional strategies. Those cities and towns that promote film or music industry activities use the popular culture building block. Integrating art into community economic development is also becoming popular. With proper application, art and related activities can provide the basis of a community's concept marketing strategy.

Table 1.1
List of Profile Communities

Popular Culture
Bellows Falls, Vermont
Loveland, Colorado
Toppenish, Washington
Winterset, Iowa
Roslyn, Washington
Mountain View, Arkansas
Eunice, Louisiana
Branson, Missouri

Corporate
Austin, Minnesota
Hershey, Pennsylvania
Newark, Ohio

Retail
Boaz, Alabama
Manchester, Vermont
Vacaville, California
Havana, Florida
Walnut, Iowa
Wooster, Ohio

Tradition
Cape May, New Jersey
Nachitoches, Louisiana
Eureka Springs, Arkansas
Fredericksburg, Texas
Solvang, California
New Glarus, Wisconson

Surrealism
Mount Dora, Florida
Helen, Georgia
Holland, Michigan
Roswell, New Mexico
Valentine, Nebraska

Figure 1.1
Geographic Distribution of Profiled Communities

Corporate "icons," such as those readily identified with a private brand, can also provide the foundation for a community to develop a concept marketing strategy. Several vignettes of communities that have successfully integrated corporate iconicism into their marketing plans are presented in Chapter 3.

Chapter 4 continues the exploration of concept marketing by focusing on those communities that have built approaches on retail-based developments and activities. Recreational shopping as an economic development target is the primary focus of communities' marketing efforts in this category. Outlet shopping as well as specialty, or themed, retail developments comprise the basis of this approach. This chapter provides examples of outlet-based development and antiquing and other specialty retail development.

Historic preservation as a community economic development strategy is gaining more attention as cultural and heritage awareness, appreciation, and tourism-based activities are increasing. Chapter 5 illustrates how communities can develop a complete marketing and development concept by utilizing historic preservation and cultural resources. The first section presents vignettes of several communities that have effectively built entire community development strategies around historic preservation. The second section explores ethnicity as the basis for constructing concept marketing approaches. Cultural resources have been creatively positioned to promulgate economic development outcomes.

The use of physical image and design to create, or re-create, a particular ambience is outlined in Chapter 6. Surrealism best captures the flavor of this concept marketing approach. Ranging literally from the creation of town facades that never existed to incorporating some element of historical significance to recapture past architectural aspects of the built environment, surrealism as a marketing approach holds the potential to be highly effective.

After exploring each of the four concept approaches, Chapter 7 examines the factors that are required to implement and succeed with community concept marketing. Clever concept approaches require more than just the initial creativity in construction; it requires effective organizations, policies, and programs for implementation. An assessment of practices is provided, indicating the most effective uses of concept marketing approaches.

2

Popular Culture

Some cities and towns embrace various aspects of popular culture to develop marketing approaches. Popular culture runs the gamut from music, filmmaking, and the visual arts. Incorporating these elements into a community marketing concept can be speculative and, at the same time, very exciting. Communities are finding that the entertainment industry—whether production or performance—can play a vital role in stimulating quality community economic development.

WHERE ART THOU?

The visual arts as an industry and as an economic development strategy have only recently been accepted as congruent concepts. Although art has been integrated into urban design throughout history, it is now viewed as an element to create an environment—"the city as an art object" (Goodey 1994:155). Communities throughout the United States have found that the arts can play a crucial and valuable role in their local economic development efforts. The effects are both indirect and direct (R. Phillips 1998). The indirect effects of incorporating the arts into a development and marketing strategy are inherently acceptable: increasing the amenities and aesthetics of a community to enhance its overall image and consequently attracting additional growth and development. The more evident direct effects include increased economic activity in jobs, sales, and public revenues.

The arts as related to community economic development and subsequent marketing efforts can be defined as: (1) an industry comprised of individuals, institutions, and organizations functioning as businesses interrelated with other local and regional businesses; (2) wide-ranging to specific cultural amenities; and (3) cultural education, tools, policies, and processes (National Conference of State Legislators 1987:138). Some communities incorporate more than one of these definitions into their concept marketing; others focus on one to build their concept; for example, an emphasis on public artworks to attract tourist revenues. States too are realizing the benefits of incorporating arts into overall economic development strategy, reflected by such actions as declarations in strategic development plans to promote and develop cultural amenities and artistic expressions (Hoke 1996).

A highly applied aspect of incorporating art into community economic development strategy is emerging: development of arts business incubators. Defined in this context, an arts business incubator is a program designed to encourage the start-up and development of arts-related small business enterprises (R. Phillips 1998). Some communities are finding that they can convert underutilized buildings, such as warehouses or schools, into studio and related uses. Keeping the costs of the space low and providing support services to make it affordable and feasible for artist entrepreneurs to set up business. New Orleans, Louisiana, has the most well-known arts incubator program, sponsored primarily by the Entergy Corporation, a utility provider in the region. Opened in May 1992, the Entergy Arts Business Center provides support services and rental space at affordable prices to individual artists and arts organizations. Support services are key to the success of the program, which include monthly business forums and workshops open to the artist community, and an entrepreneurial series that provides business planning, marketing, and other development assistance to low- and moderate-income artist entrepreneurs (Hoke 1996).

Jerome, Arizona, incorporates art in the public realm to encourage economic development outcomes by developing its concept as an artist community. Another example, Steubenville, Ohio, has painted extensive murals throughout its historic downtown, some of which depict the history of the town while others have different inspirations. The murals attract visitors to the city, where tours and interpretation are provided. Another community, Toppenish, Washington—"The City of Murals"—has aggressively used murals to integrate cultural elements of the city's past with public art. Other communities use statuary and sculptures as a method of increasing interest in their communities. Loveland, Colorado, with several hundred sculptures, is an example of this art-based approach. Bellows Falls, Vermont, has successfully built its concept marketing approach on art using an integrated approach that encompasses a wide variety of arts and related programs and activities.

LIGHTS, CAMERAS, ACTION: FILMMAKING AS A CONCEPT BASIS

Aggressive recruitment of the filmmaking industry by communities, regions, and states has increased in popularity, particularly during the 1990s. "States have recognized that this is a viable form of economic development," declared the president of the Association of Film Commissioners International, based in Los Angeles (quoted in Coolidge 1995:1). Many state economic development departments now have budgets and staff for marketing their state's locations as potential sites to film companies. Kansas's Travel and Tourism Development Division spends $1.2 million annually to promote film production and tourism in the state—the tourism industry generates a $2.5 billion impact per year and employs 46,000 (*The Economist* 1999). The competition is fierce, with myriad incentives offered to lure producers; it is not uncommon for state governors to "become pitchman on solicitation missions to the west coast" (Hollinger 1990:69). In 1997, Wisconsin's governor hosted a party for native-born writers, actors, producers, and directors in North Hollywood to promote filmmaking in the state (McGarry 1997). Filmmaking brings large amounts of money to the location during television or film production. South Dakota received a $12 million infusion from the film *Dances with Wolves* (Hornaday 1994). Each episode of a television series can generate hundreds of thousands of direct expenditures into a local economy—the series *Homicide* added about $700,000 per episode to Baltimore's economy (Sullivan 1994). In high production states, the stakes are even higher: in 1996, New York benefited from direct expenditures of $2.2 billion from film and television production (Roman 1997).

Besides the attraction of large expenditures in local economies, television and film production is desirable as a low-cost, clean industry. "Movie production also requires only a small initial investment (from the host community) . . . states don't have to build new infrastructure—roads or sewage systems—as they do for other development projects, such as those for the automobile industry" (Coolidge 1995:1). Filmmaking is generally considered to be sensitive to the environment and to have low impact on the surrounding area.

Cities have entered the competition with film office staffs vying for attention from film producers. The Tucson, Arizona, Film Office markets locations not only for westerns, but also for contemporary productions (Fiscus 1991). With tens of millions of dollars at stake, the community treats the recruitment of film productions with as much importance as recruiting major manufacturing facilities. Savannah, Georgia, has learned about the benefits of film production—according to the Savannah Film Commission, the city accrued $8.3 million in direct expenditures in 1997 and an indirect impact of $17.6 million, using a multiplier of 2.12 (Berryman 1998:88).

Even small communities are finding that filmmaking can have dramatic impacts. Consider the experience of Bozeman, Montana (*A River Runs Through It*), or Dyersville, Iowa. In 1988, the movie *Field of Dreams* was filmed in Dyersville. Although the town of 3,500 residents did not experience a tremendously large influx of capital during the actual filming, the event created the basis for continued tourism. The Dyersville Chamber of Commerce had the foresight to buy the merchandising rights to the movie; the souvenir business resulting from this has been a boon to the organization (Hornaday 1994). The movie site, in two local farmers' fields, attracts up to 50,000 visitors per year (Hornaday 1994:16). This chapter includes vignettes of two small communities in which film or television production has played a major role in developing a marketing concept: Winterset, Iowa, and Roslyn, Washington.

However, all outcomes of filmmaking on a community are not necessarily positive. Some have found that it is disruptive to the community, particularly in regards to traffic flow (especially in a small town). When historic Canton, Mississippi, was selected as the filming site for the movie *A Time to Kill*, John Grisham's first novel, there were mixed reactions. Undoubtedly, the economic impact was welcomed in this town of 11,000, yet it was unclear how the film's sensitive topic of racial conflict would impact the southern town with 70 percent black residents (Yellin 1995). It turned Canton into a tourist attraction, and the City of Canton still offers tours of the filming sites and the antebellum architecture of its town square (City of Canton 2000).

DO YOU HEAR MUSIC?

In addition to film production, another entertainment factor has always served to attract tourists—music. Especially when combined with other entertainment opportunities, music can form the basis for a community's successful concept marketing approach. One only has to look to Nashville, Tennessee, or New Orleans to gauge the widespread impact that music and related activities can have on an area. The synergy of integrating musical attractions with related activities like sales of branded merchandise and themed restaurants is being applied in communities across North America (Adler 1995). Hard Rock Café and Planet Hollywood exemplify this concept, using music as one of the integrated attractions for the experience offered to patrons. As an entertainment planning consultant described, synergy requires assembling "sufficient critical mass of different opportunities in one location" (quoted in Adler 1995:69). Some communities have built concept marketing approaches on the basis of this concept—creating a mass of opportunities based on music and related activities. Branson, Missouri, exemplifies this approach, offering a broad entertainment experience yet noted for its musical performances. The concept may be themed, in the sense that a cultural element provides the setting, such as Eunice, Louisiana's, Cajun music connection, or Mountain View, Arkansas's, folk music setting.

VISUAL ART

Art as a strategy for encouraging quality community economic development has only recently gained widespread attention. However, its role in community development has roots in the City Beautiful Movement that began in the late 1890s. The concept of integrating public art, public parks and other spaces, and beautiful architecture for public buildings became highly popular for several decades. Many creations from that era provide the fodder for historic preservation work. When the era of the City Beautiful Movement ended, the willingness to incorporate public art was practically lost until the resurgence of interest almost a hundred years later.

Three communities have been selected as exemplars in developing concept marketing approaches on the basis of art and related activities. Bellows Falls, Vermont, has taken the approach of a fully integrated arts connection to overall community quality and development. Loveland, Colorado's, approach is one of public art on a large scale—literally hundreds of sculptures are interwoven throughout the city. Toppenish, Washington, has built its concept on murals that portray its western theme.

BELLOWS FALLS, VERMONT
POPULATION: 3,700
CONCEPT: ART MAKES A DIFFERENCE

Only a handful of communities truly understand the positive economic and social impacts that an arts integrated development strategy can have. Bellows Falls is one of those. The conversion from a depressed and dying former mill town to a vibrant community attracting national attention has been dramatic and impressive. The arts have been the key to this community's revitalization.

Bellows Falls has been an incorporated village since 1834 and is actually located within another town, Rockingham. It has a rich history, one that has provided a good foundation for building a revitalized economy and community. It is the home of the first chartered canal in the United States, built between 1791 and 1802 to bypass the falls—it still runs through the village. The area attracted Native Americans for centuries before European settlers, as evidenced by prehistoric petroglyphs carved into rocks near the Connecticut River (Marcel 2000). Other features include Victorian era architecture, complete with a distinctive town square lined with red brick buildings.

During the 1800s, Bellows Falls grew as a result of railroad activities and later, paper mills. By the late 1980s, the village was in serious economic decline, with the once vibrant brick factories vacant and crumbling, and the Victorian houses subdivided into apartments (Marcel 2000:B9). The downtown railroad hotel was closed, the majority of storefronts were empty, and only one track in the large rail yard was used. Quoting the writer of the book *Bellows Falls*, the village was described this way in 1997:

Developmentally stalled since the Great Depression, and reduced to being the bedroom to almost every other town within a half-hour's commute, it has a dour and pessimistic self-image out of all proportion to its size. . . . A museum of glories past, the name Bellows Falls had become a statewide joke, solely equated with failure. (quoted in Marcel 2000)

A few short years later, Bellows Falls has been upheld as a model for community revitalization. So much change has occurred that the Vermont Community Development Association held a day-long conference in 2000 to "showcase the village as a 'prime example' of a community using creative ideas, the arts, cooperative local citizen efforts and wide variety of funding sources to revitalize itself" (R. Smith 2000:B1).

Developing the Concept

In 1997, several events occurred that started the process of changing Bellows Falls in motion. One was the formation of a grass-roots community group called Our Town, whose first project was to restore the historic clock tower that had not operated in decades (Keese 2000). Over $10,000 was raised to restore the clock as symbol of the village's commitment to its revitalization. During this time, a community group, the Front Porch Theatre Company, was formed (Keese 2000:81). Robert McBride, an artist from New York who first visited the village in the early 1980s, founded the Rockingham Arts and Museum Project (RAMP). This community-based organization has as its mission statement:

RAMP is intent on developing awareness of the arts, creating vitality in the community with the arts and demonstrating that the arts favorably impact the local economy. Success of the program relies on developing effective partnerships. The theme *is* Art Makes a Difference! (Rockingham Art and Museum Project 2000a).

RAMP has been credited with prompting the village into action and taking charge of their future, rather than being victimized by hard economic conditions. Live performances are held throughout the community, generating interest in the arts and building community morale. Activities include the Bread and Puppet Theater (a $4,000 Opportunity Grant from the Vermont Arts Council helped finance this event); a spring series of music, Flying Under the Radar; and the Yellow Barn Music Festival (Rockingham Art and Museum Project 2000a:2). RAMP does more than organize and coordinate arts events. It integrates art into overall community development in a manner that builds support for the arts through infrastructure improvement and other activities. For example, RAMP served on a committee to complete the application for downtown designation through The Vermont Downtown Development Act. In December of 1999, Bellows Falls became the ninth community in the state to receive official Downtown Designation, which helps to promote revitalization efforts (Lockwood 2000). McBride has been described as a "tireless arts promoter with a knack for bringing people and resources together (with) an unshakable conviction that Bellows Falls is a treasure just waiting to be discovered" (Keese 2000). His energy and leadership have prompted literally dozens of projects and cultural events throughout the community.

The underlying conviction for the community-wide revitalization effort is that the arts are key to revitalizing the village. While arts events alone are not enough, it is the integration of the arts into overall community development strategy and planning that has had a remarkable impact on Bellows Falls.

Outcomes

One of the most exciting projects that RAMP and other organizations participated in was the renovation of historic Exner Block. Built in the 1870s, the pressed tin structure is considered one of the state's important architectural features (Vermont Arts Council 2000). Remaining unused for decades, the Exner Block now provides affordable space for artist studios and living space, with ten apartments and six storefronts. The funding required a creative mix of public and private sources, bringing together more than $1 million in tax credits from local banks; $400,000 from federal sources; and $400,000 from the state of Vermont (Rockingham Arts and Museum Project 2000b).

Other projects include the painting of a 32' x 40' mural of a representation of historic downtown Bellows Falls circa 1890. The project cost $15,000 and various sources of funding have been obtained, including a $5,000 grant from the Vermont Arts Council (R. Smith 2000). RAMP also succeeded in securing $34,000 worth of funding from the National Endowment for the Arts and the Mid-Atlantic Arts Foundation to sponsor the Artists & Communities program to fund four-month residencies of artists from other parts of the United States (Rockingham Arts and Museum Project 2000b).

Again, the creativity exhibited by Bellows Falls citizens and community-based organizations has made a tremendous difference in building the concept and in revitalization efforts. The willingness to integrate arts into overall community development strategy and planning is key to the efforts and is reflected in a variety of projects, such as the following:

- Enticing the 35,000 visitors that come to Bellows Falls to ride the Green Mountain Flyer train to explore the downtown. They currently congregate at the railroad station on the nearby island. It is proposed to link the island with a pathway and bridge to the downtown for a scenic trail highlighting historic points of interest such as the grist mill, the petroglyphs, and the Victorian architecture. A major project for construction of a multimodal transportation center was funded with federal sources, with a $1.5 million grant.
- Installing historic style street lights for downtown, using funding of $98,000 secured from a variety of sources.
- Completing the Waypoint Interpretive Center as part of the Connecticut River Scenic Byway Project. The village was awarded $466,000 for this project.
- Restoring the Windham Hotel. Funds have been secured to purchase and stabilize the building, and the village is seeking a purchaser.

In retrospect, the transformation that has occurred in Bellows Falls from 1997 to 2001 is dramatic. The Bellows Falls experience in utilizing the arts as a basis for community development is extremely positive and serves as an inspiration for other areas. Photographs 2.1 and 2.2 provide views of art incorporated into the community.

Photograph 2.1
Art in the Street, Bellows Falls, Vermont

Courtesy of Beliz Brother, "Artists Create Communities, National Endowment for the Arts Millennium Artist."

Photograph 2.2
Art Galleries, Bellows Falls, Vermont

Courtesy of Beliz Brother, "Artists Create Communities, National Endowment for the Arts Millennium Artist."

LOVELAND, COLORADO
POPULATION: 45,000
CONCEPT: A WORK OF ART

Loveland, gateway to Rocky Mountain National Park, is located forty-five miles north of Denver in Larimer County. Plotted in 1877 on a wheat field near the new tracks of the Colorado Central Railroad, Loveland was named for retired Army general and railroad president, W. A. H. Loveland (Loveland Chamber of Commerce 2000). A wood and brick railroad station was soon built; the structure presently stands in its original form. Agriculture was the primary impetus for development of the rail town, as well as a shipping point for lumber and stone from nearby quarries.

Arts began to play a role in Loveland's development early in its history. In 1884, an opera house was constructed to provide entertainment. In 1919, the Rialto Theater was constructed in art noveau style complete with over 1,000 wooden seats, dressing rooms, an orchestra pit, and a balcony (City of Loveland 2000). After 1947, the theater declined and the building became vacant. The Loveland Downtown Development Authority began efforts to revitalize downtown in 1987 and targeted the Rialto for restoration. The City of Loveland now operates the Rialto as a community performing arts center, and the building has been added to the National Register of Historic Places (City of Loveland 2000). Arts have continued to serve as a cornerstone in the community in a variety of ways, all of which have impacted development and quality of life in Loveland.

Developing the Concept

Loveland, because of its name, first developed a concept of a valentine capital. In 1947, a valentine card remailing program was initiated which has continued to the present time. However, the concept is not the dominant component of community economic development efforts. Because of its proximity to Denver, several large corporations have established operations there, as well as a few local publishing enterprises that have grown substantially (Couch 1999). There is another reason, too, why corporations and others locate in Loveland: the community thrives on art. Here, the connection between the arts and community economic development is palpable.

The following description of Loveland in its 2001 Relocation and Visitor's Guide captures its focus on the arts:

The arts are abundantly heard and seen in Downtown including concerts in Peters Park during the summer, music and theater outdoors at the Foote Lagoon, and performances at the historic Rialto Theater by visiting musical or theatrical companies, as well as Loveland's own Choral Society, Chamber Orchestra, and community theater groups. The Loveland Museum/Gallery hosts many prestigious shows and exhibits throughout the year, and the various painters' and sculptors' galleries are unrivaled. Public art can be seen throughout the downtown and Civic Center. As noted in Richard Villani's recent publication, *The 100 Best Small Art Towns in America*, Loveland richly deserves its #8 rating, and many of the reasons for that distinction can be found downtown. (Loveland Chamber of Commerce 2000:16)

In 1983, a group of citizens and business owners began to consider the arts as a potential force for community redevelopment, given the growing artists' community forming in Loveland. They realized that underneath the aluminum facades and paint, a strong base of historic properties existed. The ability to revitalize downtown buildings as space for art and cultural activities was the key: by 1989, twenty-five full and part-time artists had studios and residences downtown, with more expressing interest (Arvidson 1989). Since that time, many artists have chosen Loveland as a place to establish a studio and home. Loveland continued its commitment to the arts, and in 1985, became the first Colorado city to pass an ordinance designating 1 percent of the city's capital construction projects of $50,000 or more for the purchase of art (Loveland Visitors Center 2000).

The City of Loveland has helped encourage the arts in other ways, too. There are twenty-five public parks, and many of these house pieces of public art. The Benson Park Sculpture Garden houses more than forty pieces of sculpture. The Loveland Museum and Gallery, operated by the city since 1945, completed an expansion project in 1992 and received accreditation from the American Association of Museums in 1990 (Loveland Visitors Center 2000:3).

Outcomes

The Art in Public Places ordinance has had a positive impact on Loveland. As of 1999, 163 pieces of art (many statues) were located throughout the community and the economic impact has been very positive: more artists have moved to Loveland and rehabilitated downtown buildings; businesses that ship or install or are otherwise related to artwork have established enterprises; and the number of tourists has grown dramatically (Florida Planning 1999). The value of the public art collection is valued at over $2 million (Loveland Visitors Center 2000: 175). Many of the art pieces are by nationally and internationally renowned artists and have been donated from private sources.

In the late 1980s, a community organization, with help from public and private entities, began the annual Sculpture in the Park event. This activity has helped focus attention on Loveland's numerous works of art, as well as the city's resident artists. In 1991, the Loveland Sculpture Group was formed to further expand opportunities for Loveland's sculptures (Heitman 2001). A summary of this nonprofit organization's goals is: (1) host an annual sculpture show that brings together sculptors from around the world; (2) make the show appealing to a wide audience to encourage interest in sculpture; (3) use any profits from the show to fund sculpture projects for the City of Loveland and to establish a fund for the study of the visual arts (Loveland Sculpture Group 2001).

Photograph 2.3
Art in the Park, Loveland, Colorado

Photograph 2.4
One of Many Sculptures in Loveland, Colorado

Courtesy of Loveland Chamber of Commerce and Visitor's Center and Fabrice Photography, Loveland, Colorado.

The event, the Annual Loveland Sculpture Invitational Show, has become the largest assembled group of sculptors and sculpture in the United States. Over 300 artists from the United States and other countries display over 3,500 sculptures. In 1999, $20,000 in proceeds from the show were donated to support art education in Loveland area schools (Loveland Sculpture Group 2000:1).

Loveland has become known as "A Work of Art," given the numerous sculptures and art activities that are interwoven throughout the city. A local civic organization described the relationship between art and the city: "Loveland artists thrive on their community's support and the community thrives on its art" (Loveland Visitors Center 2000). Photographs 2.3 and 2.4 give examples of Loveland's works of art.

TOPPENISH, WASHINGTON
POPULATION: 7,500
CONCEPT: THE CITY OF MURALS—WHERE THE WEST STILL LIVES

Toppenish, the home of the Yakama Indian Nation, is located forty miles from the million acre Columbia Basin. Equidistant from Seattle, Spokane, and Portland, Oregon, Toppenish is positioned within the verdant Lower Yakima Valley. Vineyards, fruit orchards, and hops, berry, and vegetable farms are interspersed in the rolling hills of the valley, providing a striking backdrop for the town.

Located in the area is the Yakama Nation Cultural Heritage Center. The center includes a museum housing exhibits portraying the story of the Yakama Indian People; a replica of a winterlodge meeting hall and a library with a collection of tribal papers and books. In 1998, the Yakama Nation opened the Legends Casino, a 51,000 square foot facility decorated with a western outdoor theme (FitzSimmons 1998). The décor complements Toppenish's concept as a western town, which has been overseen since 1983 by a design review board for ensuring coordination of western themed facades and architectural details (Brooks-Pittman 2000). For decades, the Toppenish Pow-Wow and Rodeo has been held over the July 4th weekend. This event attracts thousands of visitors to Toppenish. Additionally, several smaller Mexican rodeos are held during the summer, featuring rodeo performers dressed in traditional Mexican attire (City of Toppenish 2000).

Developing the Concept

Toppenish's economy was declining by the 1980s; an experience repeated throughout the United State's rural communities dependent on agriculture. Despite a regional rodeo that attracted visitors during the event and a western themed town, Toppenish was not a tourist destination. It would take something more, and that was discovered in the late 1980s when a group of concerned citizens and business owners decided to form the Toppenish Mural Society for preserving the culture and history of the town's western heritage. Yet, it was intended to do more than preserve culture: it was designed to revitalize downtown with murals. In June of 1989, the first mural was painted on the side of a downtown building as part of the first Mural-in-a-Day event (Kerby 2000). The mural was designed by an artist from Yakima who supervised fifteen noted western artists' collaborative work to complete the scene in one day.

What happened next is impressive. The Toppenish Mural Society, a nonprofit organization, raises funds each year to paint more murals. Costing thousands each, they cover the costs via selling memberships in the Society from $20 to $500 or more to citizens, organizations, and businesses throughout the Yakama Valley as well as soliciting contributions (Brooks-Pittman 2000). Because of their commitment and the support from the Toppenish Chamber of Commerce and the City, numerous murals have been painted throughout downtown. A Visitors Welcome Center was established which houses the Society, the Toppenish Rodeo & Livestock Association, and the Toppenish Chamber of Commerce offices. All of these groups, with the Yakama Nation, coordinate efforts to market Toppenish as The City of Murals.

The quality of the murals is outstanding. Each year, artists' ideas are submitted to be judged on the basis of historical accuracy and high artistic standards, and must reflect the time period 1850 to 1950 (Flint Publishing, Inc. 2000:58). Only a few murals are selected each year, with the painting season running from April through the end of October.

Outcomes

Tourism has become a major industry for Toppenish, since the inception of painting of the murals in 1989. By 2000, between 25,000 and 30,000 visitors per year journey to the town to view fifty-seven murals (Kerby 2000). Special events and festivals have been established to showcase the murals and draw additional tourists to town. These include the Western Art Show during a three-day period in August that uses the downtown Railroad Park as an art gallery; during the same time, the Yakima Valley Rail and Transportation Show is held at the restored rail depot's museum (Brooks-Pittman 2000). Also during the summer, the Yakima Valley Concert Band performs outdoor concerts.

The results for Toppenish of a concept marketing approach based on arts, in this case, murals, has been extremely positive. The mural painting has drawn national, and even some international, attention to Toppenish, resulting in increased tourism. The murals have had positive outcomes other than economic—they have served to increase pride in the town and stimulated interest in preserving its culture and heritage.

FILMMAKING

Filmmaking and television production can be an attractive economic development strategy. Results can be mixed, however, depending on the duration of the filming and the attitudes of citizens towards the influx of equipment, crews, props, and casts into their community. Two very different experiences are presented via the vignettes of Winterset, Iowa, and Roslyn, Washington. Winterset was the location of the film, *The Bridges of Madison County*, and Roslyn was the site of filming the television series *Northern Exposure* for several years.

WINTERSET, IOWA
POPULATION: 4,768
CONCEPT: MADISON COUNTY

Madison County was the setting for the best-selling novel by Robert James Waller, *The Bridges of Madison County*, which was adapted for the screen and filmed entirely in the area in 1995. Why Winterset and Madison County? The main reason is that the county was home to nineteen covered bridges, of which six remain. All are listed on the National Register of Historic Places. This and the rolling hills of rich farmland provided the setting for both the novel and the film.

For years, the town has held an annual Covered Bridges Festival to celebrate its architectural treasures. Founded in 1849, Winterset features a historic town square with several turn-of-the-century buildings. It also has some claim to fame as the birthplace of actor John Wayne. The cottage where Wayne was born, restored to its 1907 appearance, displays memorabilia and attracts a number of people each year (Marks 1995). Yet, it was not until publication of the novel and release of the movie that Winterset became a major tourist destination. In 1995, over 120,000 tourists attended the annual festival and 157 bus tours were scheduled for the four weeks before the festival (*The Economist* 1995). Prior to the appearance of the novel and the film, attendance was far less—in 1992, it was 50,000 (Dorsey 1993).

Developing the Concept

When Winterset realized that the popular novel would be made into a movie and would be filmed on location in Madison County, they looked to Dyersville, about 200 miles away, for advice. Dyersville was the site of the film *Field of Dreams* and had become one of the top tourism sites in Iowa, attracting up to 50,000 visitors annually seven years after the film was made (King 1995). They followed Dyersville's lead, and the Madison County Chamber of Commerce obtained the exclusive right to sell merchandise based on the film. They had previously negotiated rights to sell t-shirts based on the novel's cover (Applegate 1993). The Chamber sells a variety of merchandise via mail order and on-site that feature the novel and movie, as well as the history of the area.

The Madison County Chamber of Commerce plays the leading role in marketing Winterset and the county as the venue for the novel and the movie. Support for marketing comes from other organizations that feature attractions and from retail and service businesses in the area. About $30,000 to $40,000 is spent annually for all marketing efforts (Cermak 2001).

Outcomes

The impact of the novel and its filming on Madison County has been dramatic. While the volume of tourists has declined from its peak of 37,000 to about 15,000 in 2001, the concept still attracts income, interest, and tourists to Madison County (Cermak 2001). The Iowa Department of Economic Development's Tourism Division conducted a longitudinal study of the impact of travel on Iowa counties. Table 2.1 illustrates the continued effect of tourism on Madison County and the success of its concept marketing approach. As seen in Table 2.1, the level of expenditures by tourists in the county has increased, counter to the common conviction that once filming is complete the levels of expenditures decline. While the absolute numbers of tourists visiting Winterset has declined since 1994, the amount of expenditures has not. This is likely due to the continued efforts of the county to develop more attractions and support services to retain visitors in the area for a longer period of time. Another indicator of a community's long-term tourist appeal is to measure the tax receipts at the local level. Table 2.2 provides a summary of the tax revenues collected during the time frame, 1994 to 1999. As seen, revenues have actually increased, rather than declined.

Winterset and Madison County have benefited from the inflow of tourists and expenditures. Its concept marketing approach, building on the novel and film that bears its name, has been quite successful and has enjoyed longevity.

ROSLYN, WASHINGTON
POPULATION: 1,017
CONCEPT: CICELY, ALASKA'S SISTER CITY

At an altitude of 2,366 feet in the Cascade Mountain range, Roslyn *could* pass for a small Alaskan town. And it did, enough to convince the producers of the television series *Northern Exposure* to film on location from 1991 to 1995.

Table 2.1
Tourist Expenditures for Madison County

Year	Amount (in millions)
1999	$5.94
1998	$5.65
1997	$5.72
1996	$5.65
1995	$5.48
1994	$5.29

Source: Iowa Department of Economic Development 2000.

Table 2.2
Local Tax Revenues for Madison County

Year	Amount
1999	$600,000
1998	$600,000
1997	$460,000
1995	$500,000
1994	$400,000

Source: Iowa Department of Economic Development 2000.

Roslyn has a tumultuous history. Built by the Northern Pacific Coal Company in 1886, the population of the community reached 6,000 during the early part of the twentieth century, producing a million tons of coal annually (Ricks 1993). Named for the New York hometown of a mining executive's sweetheart, Roslyn housed twenty-four saloons during its height (Kauffman 1992). Timber played a role too; although both the mining and timber industries began to decline, and by 1962, the last coal mine closed. The town's population dwindled to less than 900, and the economic future did not seem very bright for Roslyn.

Because of its relatively isolated location just east of Snoqualmie Pass (which sometimes closes during severe winter weather), Roslyn's turn-of-the-century architecture and character remained relatively intact. In 1987, the entire community was listed in the National Register of Historic Places due to its preserved architecture (Winchell 1992). Fortunately, this was the ambience that producers were seeking when they wanted to replicate a small Alaskan town for the *Northern Exposure* series.

Developing the Concept

The concept for Roslyn was "inherited," and not explicitly promoted by Roslyn, although the town has gained from the exposure generated by the on-site filming. Roslyn had a tumultuous relationship at first with the production company, and several issues arose that caused concern among some of the town's citizens. They were concerned with the increased volume of traffic that interfered with daily life, such as checking their mail boxes at the post office, increasing property prices, and the attitudes of the production crew and cast, which numbered over a hundred (Di Salvatore 1993). Over one hundred citizens signed a petition objecting to the presence of the film crew and the disruption caused in Roslyn. It was not an easy transition for the town or the production crew during the early days of filming. Later, the production company made efforts to smooth over some of the tension by donating a fire truck to the town, sponsoring a 10-K race, distributing holiday baskets, and other activities (Di Salvatore 1993:46). The town's leadership was always supportive, recognizing the filming as a much needed boost to the economy of Roslyn. The mayor of Roslyn at the time explained that the town had gone through tough economic times, losing much of its population, and that the economic boost from the filming was welcome, as welcome as any industry that would consider Roslyn (Di Salvatore 1993:45). The difficulties seemed to pass, and by the end of the filming tenure, Roslyn had accepted *Northern Exposure*.

In 1995, after the filming of the series ceased, the Roslyn Business Association was formed by members of the community to promote the welfare of Roslyn. They sponsor several special events and festivals, such as an antique car show to spur tourism to the area (Friends of Roslyn 2001). Realizing that the influx of visitors and money into Roslyn was slowing, the town started investigating alternatives to revitalize its economy.

Outcomes

There are visible reminders of the days when filming took place: The Brick Tavern; Central Sundries, known as RuthAnne's General Store; Cicely's Gifts in Dr. Fleischman's office building; and the Roslyn Café. The Brick's reputation actually predates the show, having opened in 1889. It is the oldest standing tavern in the state of Washington and still houses much of the original furnishings and fixtures (Ricks 1993).

During the filming of the series and for a few years afterwards, Roslyn experienced a surge in tourism. The Roslyn Museum, housing artifacts from its days as a coal mining town, as well as information on the television series, reported a dramatic increase in visitors. Before the series began, 2,000 to 3,000 people per year visited the museum, in 1992, 24,000 visitors signed the guest book (Kauffman 1992). Eleven new businesses opened in Roslyn when the series began, and 100 new jobs were added (Kauffman 1992:6). Eight extra people were added to the staff at The Brick to accommodate the increase in business, and revenues from local sales taxes increased by nearly 70 percent in 1991 (Brannon 1992). The town of Roslyn charged $100 a day for a filming permit, and the $5,500 collected during the first season was added to the general fund (Brannon 1992:61).

Several years after filming ceased, the interest in Roslyn from *Northern Exposure* fans declined. Some of the stores that had opened to serve the tourists closed, and tourist-related activities were relatively quiet. But the story and the impact of the series goes on. Beginning in 1999, the Moose Days festival, held each July, is organized and conducted by fans of *Northern Exposure*. The fans conceived the idea via the Internet, forming a group called Friends of Roslyn, a volunteer effort. Friends of Roslyn is a nonprofit organization with the mission of establishing and maintaining events to encourage the support of arts and educational programs in Roslyn and surrounding areas (Friends of Roslyn 2001). All proceeds from Moose Days activities are given to charitable and civic groups in Roslyn. From its first festival in 1999, $10,000 was earned and distributed to the Roslyn Library, the chamber of commerce, and other community groups (Friends of Roslyn 2001:3). The funding also helped establish the Northern Lights Theater group.

The Cle Elum/Roslyn Chamber of Commerce reported that it does not do much marketing on the basis of *Northern Exposure*. The reason? "We do not advertise the specific element of the filming, because it is already known. We get "free" advertising due to reruns of the series," reported the chamber director (Moen 2001). The future seems to hold other plans that may revive more interest in Roslyn's days as Cicely, Alaska: a master planned community, the Morning Star Resort Complex, is being proposed for the area (Strand 2001). This could have a dramatic impact on all the communities in the area and would likely focus attention once again on Roslyn as a tourist venue.

Final analysis? The filming of *Northern Exposure* resuscitated the stagnant economy of an isolated small town. The old adage, all good things must come to an end, holds particular relevance in this case, for when filming ceased, the economic boost declined. Yet, the experience put Roslyn on the nation's map and provided the impetus for the community to consider its options to encourage economic development, such as forming the Roslyn Business Association and developing special events and festivals to renew interest in the town. As a catalyst for economic development, if nothing else, *Northern Exposure* can be considered a positive experience for Roslyn.

MUSIC

Music has transformative powers, or so it seems when communities build concept marketing approaches around it. The following three communities certainly think so, given the outcomes they have achieved as a result of incorporating music into their development strategies. Mountain View, Arkansas, has capitalized on its rich heritage of folk music to develop itself into an entertainment destination. The surging interest during the last several years in Cajun, or Acadian, music has helped Eunice, Louisiana, build its concept as the Cajun capital. Perhaps the most well-recognized community utilizing a marketing concept based on music is Branson, Missouri. Noted for its astounding number of theaters and live musical performances, Branson has developed itself into an entertainment mecca.

MOUNTAIN VIEW, ARKANSAS
POPULATION: 2,697
CONCEPT: FOLK MUSIC CAPITAL

Its isolated location in the Ozark hills of North Central Arkansas has not prevented Mountain View from becoming a tourist destination. The beautiful setting of the Ozarks has served as the venue for musicians to perform throughout the years. Built in 1923, the Stone County Courthouse stands in the center of the Mountain View town square and becomes the site where musicians gather almost nightly to play traditional folk music, hence the name Folk Music Capital (Shipman 2000b).

Located seventeen miles away are Blanchard Caverns, a major Arkansas attraction. The caverns are protected and maintained by the United States Forest Service; tours are offered to approximately 100,000 visitors per year. Mountain View has benefited from the proximity of this major tourist attraction, and pulls some of the Blanchard Caverns visitors to its venues.

Developing the Concept

In 1962, the first Arkansas Folk Festival was held in Mountain View. From that time onward, the annual event has grown in popularity and renown. The three-day springtime event includes musical performances, historical displays, an arts and crafts show, and other festivities. The festival grew from the tradition of people getting together in the Ozarks to play music, dance, and play games. Limited resources and transportation made gathering with family and friends the most feasible form of entertainment in days past (Shipman 2000a). Between 25,000 and 30,000 people per year attend the festival that features bluegrass and folk music complete with dancing on the courthouse square (*Stone County Leader* 2000).

The musicians and the community provided the impetus for the festival. This account from a newspaper article in 1964 illustrates the desire of the community to preserve its musical heritage:

Situated near the southern border of the Ozark National Forest, Mountain View is making a bid to become the folk music center of the state. It has a running start, because the kind of music played and sung is truly representative of that practiced by pioneers of Arkansas— from the heritage of "The Arkansas Traveler" to "Old Joe Clark," "Wildwood Flower," "Going up Cripple Creek," and old favorite religious hymns. There is no pay for performing, no charge for admission. It is simply a desire of people to play and listen to "good old mountain music." . . . These people, about 300 strong, are preserving Arkansas folk music by their attendance and participation each Friday night in the hootenanny in the courtroom of the stone County Courthouse at Mountain View. (Rush 1964:1)

Another influence on the folk music development concept was the influx of young people interested in folk music and back to nature living, or as local residents referred to them, "flower children" (Shipman 2000a). In the 1972 festival, the crowds were so large that the town could not accommodate them; it was estimated that as many as 100,000 people attended (Shipman 2000a:21).

Later, the Ozark Folk Center State Park became involved with the festival, as did the Committee of 100, a group formed to protect Ozark culture and its heritage (Burgett 2000). During the same time that the festival was first organized, the Ozark Foothills Handicraft Guild was formed. Its goal has been to revive and promote traditional Ozark crafts. In 1974, a craft sales shop and offices were built by the Guild close to Mountain View (Shipman 2000a). Annual shows attract many tourists, and the Guild has grown to include gifted artisans from all of Arkansas' seventy-five counties.

Outcomes

Mountain View has achieved its goal of becoming the Folk Music Capital, a claim that few dispute. Sales tax revenues have increased due to the growing number of tourists and opportunities for expenditures. In 1998, Mountain View collected $601,000 in sales tax revenues, up from $586,000 the prior year (City of Mountain View 2000). Mountain View Chamber of Commerce, the Arkansas Department of Parks and Tourism, and the local government market the festival. Fees from vendors have paid for the costs of organizing and conducting the festival Shipman 2000b). The Ozark Folk Center State Park is operated by State of Arkansas and serves as a major tourist attraction throughout the year for Mountain View. The park includes living history demonstrations, musical performances, and a cultural resources center that houses a massive collection of country and folk music.

In 2000, the Arkansas Craft Guild opened it first retail outlet in downtown Mountain View. It is located in a historic building, and will revive its tradition of holding downtown craft shows during the Arkansas Folk Festival in April (*Stone County Leader* 2000). Also established in 2000 is the Stone County Historical Society's museum located in an old school building. The museum houses a collection of items of local historical interest, as well as the Society's family research and publications archives. Mountain View has also organized other events to keep visitors traveling to the community in seasons other than spring festival time. The annual Bean Fest is held in October and in addition to the food attraction (1000 pounds of beans are served with cornbread, free), musical performances and the unusual Great Arkansas Championship Outhouse Race attracts visitors from as far away as Australia (Burgett 2000). Even MTV has expressed interest in covering the event. Popularity of the Bean Fest brings as many as 40,000 attendees.

Mountain View has achieved success with its concept development. It has become a destination, based on its music, and serves as a model for other communities that desire to preserve a unique musical heritage.

EUNICE, LOUISIANA
POPULATION: 12,000
CONCEPT: PRAIRIE CAJUN CAPITAL

An alternative concept might be Bon Temp Rouler Au! Eunice is the home of Rendez-Vous Des Cajuns, a Zydeco and Cajun music radio and television show that airs every Saturday night—the Cajun version of the Grand Ole Opry. The town's rich history supports the development of their concept marketing approach built on music.

The early founders of Eunice were descendants of the Acadians, a group of people who left western France in the early 1600s and first settled in Nova Scotia. When the British expelled the Acadians from Nova Scotia, many settled in Louisiana, and the term "Cajun" was coined for these settlers. Eunice was incorporated in 1895, springing up around a railroad station in the "prairie" land of Louisiana (not the swamp, bayou, and lowland areas where many of the Acadians settled).

Plots of land were subdivided, and an auction was held to sell home and business sites. A celebration, a fais-do-do, was held that evening to commemorate the new town's founding.

Developing the Concept

In 1985, the City of Eunice bought the Liberty Theater, an old vaudeville house built in 1924 and located in the oldest part of downtown. With the advent of this occurrence, more people in Eunice became interested in their Cajun heritage, especially preserving the music, language, and culture (Moody 2000). A local musician and his wife, Marc and Ann Savoy, are largely credited with starting the initiative to build on the community's concept of Cajun music. They felt strongly that there should be a place where citizens could hear French and Cajun being spoken, as well as listen to music and dance (Moody 2000:1). In conjunction with the city, they organized the Cajun Music Show and it opened on July 12, 1987 in the Liberty Theater—all in French. There was tremendous community-wide effort, including city workers who volunteered to be stage hands and to sell tickets.

During the 1980s, Louisiana's economy was suffering from a downturn in the oil industry; many of Eunice's citizens were employed by the oil drilling and processing companies. The efforts to restore the Liberty Theater were key to revitalizing the economy and charting a new economic direction for the town. Now, it is listed on the National Register of Historic Places, and in 1986 the city was chosen to represent Louisiana as a regional center for the Southern Arts Federation (City of Eunice 2000). A grant was obtained to hire a liaison between Eunice and the Southern Arts Center, headquartered in Atlanta (Moody 2000).

The city also developed a historic district commission to oversee the revitalization of historic buildings throughout the downtown area. Several venues were developed in historic structures, including the Eunice Depot Museum built in 1894 which contains Mardi Gras memorabilia, railroad items, and other items of local significance (City of Eunice 2000).

Outcomes

Eunice has reinvigorated its economy through its musical heritage. Marketing is conducted primarily through the city, and they also receive much "free" advertising via its success. For example, the British Broadcasting Company (BBC) visits Eunice three times a year to film shows at the Liberty Theater (Moody 2000). The BBC's filming has brought many tourists from Britain to see the live performances and other area attractions. The Rendez-Vous Des Cajun radio and television show now is performed in some English and attracts numerous visitors each year.

Other attractions have developed in Eunice. The National Park Service constructed the Jean LaFitte National Historical Park & Preserve, Prairie Acadian Culture Center to tell the story of the region's French Acadian people (Hattes 1999). Cajun history, music, architecture, and language are interpreted; events such as music and Cajun cuisine demonstrations are held as well (City of Eunice 2001). The Cajun Music Hall of Fame & Museum was created to honor individuals who contributed to cajun musical heritage and includes much memorabilia and artifacts about the development of Cajun music and musicians.

Eunice's concept of the Prairie Cajun Capital has resulted in preservation of the region's heritage and culture, most notably its unique Cajun and Zydeco musical styles. Positioning music as the basis for its concept has been the key to acceptance and support within the community.

BRANSON, MISSOURI
POPULATION: 6,000
CONCEPT: LIVE ENTERTAINMENT CAPITAL OF AMERICA

How can a small town become one of the most visited overnight leisure destinations in the United States, all within the span of about fifteen years? When efforts first started to develop Branson into an entertainment mecca, population was less than 3,000 in this small southwestern Missouri city. By 1999, Branson had nearly 7 million tourists and had secured its identify as an entertainment destination. The result of both happenstance and deliberate efforts, Branson's success with its concept marketing approach is worthy of study.

Developing the Concept

Branson always enjoyed a reputation as a tourist destination because of its beautiful surroundings, including three lakes that attract visitors for recreation. In the early 1960s, one country music show opened up in Branson and was successful. But it was not until the mid-1980s when country music star Roy Clark opened a show that Branson really began to be noticed as a significant tourist destination (Noble 2001). The Branson Lakes Area Chamber of Commerce and the local convention and visitors bureau launched a marketing campaign, "Neon and Nature," to promote the music shows and the natural features of the area.

In 1992, a fortuitous marketing event occurred in Branson, the television show *60 Minutes* aired a 30-minute show on Branson. Highlighting its unique combination of neon and nature, the impact of the national exposure was dramatic. Within a short period of time, every hotel room was booked and visitors flooded Branson. The national media coverage Branson received in response to the *60 Minutes* segment was tremendous. *CBS This Morning* broadcast live shortly thereafter; *USA Weekend,* a Sunday morning magazine with 34 million readers, carried a story a few days later; *Inside Edition* aired live from Branson to two hundred U.S. markets and six foreign countries; *Larry King Live* did a broadcast from Branson; and the town was featured on *NBC Nightly News* (Butcher 1992:8). The city got another major marketing boost in 1996, when the *Live with Regis and Kathy Lee* show spent a week broadcasting from Branson (Noble 2001).

By 1994, several theaters were operating in Branson, including the Andy Williams Moon River Theater, the BoxCar Wille Theater, the Charley Pride Theater, the Cristy Lane Theater, and the Glenn Campbell Good Time Theater. The rapid growth in Branson came with a price, however. The community's infrastructure, designed for a small population, could not accommodate tens of thousands of visitors per day. The volume of traffic became overwhelming and a sales tax increase was enacted to finance road improvements (*The Economist* 1994). By 2000, $37 million had been spent on road improvements (City of Branson 2000). Water resources and wastewater infrastructure were stressed, and a $14.75 million water treatment plant was constructed to handle the demands (The American City & County 1998). Growth management will continue to be an issue for Branson. Rapid growth also resulted in overbuilding; by 1995, several theaters, restaurants, and other supporting commercial enterprises closed (Walkup 1995). By 2000, Branson seemed to have stabilized, with a balance between the number of tourists and the number of venues.

Outcomes

Most communities only dream of receiving the type of media coverage and publicity that Branson has had. Yet Branson has implemented an aggressive marketing approach to continue attracting visitors to the area. Each year, approximately $2 million is spent on advertising and marketing activities (Noble 2001). The chamber of commerce and the convention and visitors bureau manage the marketing and receive support from the business community and the City of Branson. The marketing approach is to do spot television ads in twenty-one market areas that cover up to 500 miles, and four national cable markets. The community feels that it is critical to continue to aggressively market Branson in order to compete with other entertainment-oriented communities. Nashville, in particular, took notice of Branson's rising success as a country music entertainment mecca and invested in theater renovations to brighten its attraction to tourists (Mannix 1994).

The number of tourists to Branson has increased steadily, from 3.1 million in 1986, to 4.3 million in 1991 (Butcher 1992), 5.8 million in 1994, and 7 million in 1999 (Noble 2001). By 1994, $1.5 billion worth of goods and services were sold in Branson, and sales tax revenues had increased by 76 percent (*The Economist* 1994). As of 2001, the outcomes of Branson's marketing concept have been tremendous:

- 361 restaurants
- 198 lodging facilities, with 21,000 rooms
- 7 campgrounds, with 1,467 campsite
- 47 theaters with 80 live shows
- 57,237 seats in theaters—more than New York's Broadway district
- 100 percent increase in population from 1990 to 2000

Most of these outcomes are direct results of Branson's decision to develop its concept as an entertainment capital. As of 2000, Branson was rated the 18th most visited tourist destination in the United States (*Nation's Cities Weekly* 2000). Growth is expected to continue, with a projected 48 percent increase in employment from 1998 to 2010 in Taney County, where Branson is located (Heubusch 1998:51). Branson has certainly achieved its goal of developing itself into an entertainment mecca.

SUMMARY

Popular culture, as expressed in visual art, filmmaking, and music, provides rich concept marketing approaches for communities to reinvent their economic base. It can serve as the basis for building a tremendously successful community concept marketing approach that produces many positive outcomes. At the same time, using popular culture carries a high level of risk. Consider the following description of the appallingly competitive business of building concepts on popular culture:

When towns lived by solid resources, such as wheat or coal, they were vulnerable only to market fluctuations and changes in technology. Their prosperity could last for decades. Today many American cities have yoked their star to that most fickle of resources, popular taste. And, as with any other commodity, customer loyalty is not assured. One town can always be dropped for a better one. (*The Economist* 1994:28)

Communities may find that the level of creativity and resources it takes to maintain a popular culture concept marketing approach is too high. The constant attention it requires is demanding; if this element is not considered, communities may find themselves no longer "popular." It requires vigilance and periodic reassessment of the concept approach to adjust to the market, which can change frequently.

There are several points for communities to consider, should a popular culture concept marketing approach be attempted. These include:

Approaches integrating visual arts:

- Do not think of expenditures on arts as subsidies; rather, they are investments in economic development.
- Educate the community on the benefits of integrating arts into the community development strategy.
- Target the market intensively to identify participants and tourists.

Approaches integrating music:

- Identify unique musical resources or cultural aspects that can be used for developing the concept.
- Assess the level of interest from the community in using music as a concept.
- Target the audience to match musical taste.

Approaches integrating filmmaking:

- Consider purchasing merchandising rights to television series or movies produced in the community.
- Ask for funds from production companies to help with community infrastructure needs.
- Set the filming permits at a level to support community needs and recover associated costs.
- Educate the community on both the positive benefits and negative aspects to help prevent backlash from the community.

All approaches must build community-wide support for the concept. Without wide-scale support, it will be difficult for any popular culture concept to be successful. The key is to integrate the concept approach into the overall community development planning process, whether it be a design review board or a comprehensive planning process.

3

Corporate Iconicism

Corporate culture fascinates Americans. The branding activities that have been assimilated into vernacular culture are far-reaching and pervasive. While most are content with buying products sporting corporate logos, some have gone further with entire communities adopting a corporate identity or other aspects of corporate culture as the basis for crafting a marketing concept. Transcending the company towns of times past when entire communities were constructed by corporations to serve their production interests, this type of concept marketing approach capitalizes on corporate identity. It may be deliberate or it may be the consequences of private sector actions.

Either way, one thing is certain: the appeal of corporate tourist venues is increasing dramatically. Typically co-located in the same community as the corporation's production or headquarters facilities, the corporate museum is enjoying tremendous drawing power. When Binney & Smith Inc.'s Crayola Factory museum in Easton, Pennsylvania, first opened in 1996, it drew 300,000 visitors the first year (Quintanilla 1998). Companies are finding that even facilities built for their own employees, such as Motorola Inc.'s museum in Schaumburg, Illinois, attract numerous visitors seeking to learn more of their companies. Motorola eventually had to increase its museum staff from 12 to 31 to keep up with the unexpected high volume of visitors (Quintanilla 1998:A1).

HOW'S THAT MADE?

What makes factory tours and corporate museums so appealing to Americans? Perhaps it provides some answers to a sense of curiosity people have about how things are made. The world inside a factory or its replica is mesmerizing (Daily 2000:14). As of 2000, there were 300 factory tours and corporate museums in the

United States, with more expected to be developed. Learning how items used in everyday life are manufactured—from golf balls, to tissue, to farm implements—apparently carries a high level of appeal. Food products are especially enticing, as evidenced by the popularity of such corporate venues as Hershey, Pennsylvania's Chocolate World and the increasing popularity of Austin, Minnesota, aka Spam Town, USA. Both of these communities are profiled in this chapter.

In developing venues for visitors, some companies follow the lead set by the Coca-Cola Company's World of Coca-Cola in downtown Atlanta, Georgia, located just two miles from their international headquarters. Over 9 million visitors have toured the World of Coca-Cola in the ten years since its opening in 1990. They experience complete immersion in the history, development, and nuances of the soft drink. Soda fountains dispense forty-four of the company's beverages distributed throughout the world. The tour terminates in a massive gift shop with every imaginable Coca-Cola brand merchandise available. The location of the World of Coca-Cola in downtown Atlanta has dramatically impacted revitalization efforts in that portion of the city and provided the catalyst for additional tourist-based developments in the area.

Corning, Incorporated, located in Corning, New York, began operating as the Flint Glass Works in 1868 (Gill 1999). With its brick sidewalks and historical Market Street, the city of Corning has capitalized on the location of its most famous corporate citizen to shape itself into a glass-making center. Corning, home to three hot glass studios in addition to the well-known Corning Museum of Glass, hosts nearly 500,000 visitors per year and is now the third largest tourist attraction in New York State (Dickinson 1996). However, the museum and the city have had its ups and downs. In the 1950s the museum attracted celebrities and politicians, but the museum lost its appeal by the 1980s (Royal 2000). Determined to help the community, the museum, the town, and the three counties in the area formed Corning Enterprises in 1983 to focus on community economic development with activities such as revitalizing downtown and developing a strategic plan (Royal 2000:85). Other communities can look to this successful partnership as a model of regional economic development and revitalization. Too often, small and mid-sized communities compete with nearby towns and cities for development. The more feasible approach is to partner with them and promote the entire region in order to attract and develop tourism-based and industrial activities.

Corning Incorporated also spent over $60 million to renovate the museum and expects that the newly refurbished and expanded complex will attract large numbers of tourists to Corning (Schmidt 1999). The reinvigorated museum is proof of the commitment of the company to help boost community economic development outcomes. Corning, Incorporated is an excellent example of a corporate partner, displaying private sector cooperation with the nonprofit and public sectors to build regional concept marketing approach.

DOING WHAT IT TAKES: CREATING THE CONTEXT

Not all corporations are willing to invest in local tourist attractions. So, some communities invent them. Black River Falls, Wisconsin, has proposed to build Steinhaus—a nine-story replica of a beer stein. The glass handle will house the elevator shaft; the top floor, a pub. Other attractions include 34,000 square feet of rentable space to include a museum, art gallery, and a microbrewery. This "functional sculpture" will also serve as a beer-stein shaped mall (Calamba 1996). Why look at this as a development strategy? Because larger-than-life symbolic architecture can be a major tourist attraction. Another example is Newark, Ohio, home of The Longaberger Company, the world's largest manufacturer of handwoven baskets and noted internationally for its corporate headquarters: a seven-story replica of the company's market basket. The building itself is a major tourist attraction, as well as nearby tourist venues developed by the corporation and several communities along Route 16.

One community has ventured further than others in linking itself to a corporate image: changing its name to that of a corporate brand name. Tiny Granville, North Dakota, population 270, won a promotional contest sponsored by Sazerac Co., a distributor of Dr. McGillicuddy's Imported Schnapps (Baar 1998). For the four-year period 1998–2002, Granville has changed its name to McGillicuddy City. In return, they receive $100,000, which the community will use to build a civic center. Unexpected results? A number of tourists visit McGillicuddy City, buying t-shirts, shot glasses, and drinking Schnapps at the Shady Eye Saloon (Lukas 1999). The impact of national coverage and tourists on the small town have been so positive that a member of the Granville (McGillicuddy City) Community Economic Development Board proclaimed, "We might just keep the name, for another hundred thou" (Lukas 1999:48).

However, not all dominant corporations have positive relationships with their host community. Cashmere, Washington, is a small town of 2,500 known primarily as the home of Liberty Orchards, producers of Aplets & Cotlets, a fruit confection. In 1997, Liberty Orchards presented the town with a plan to include its Aplets & Cotlets brand on road signs, the town's correspondence, and street signs (Kelley 1997). They also asked to purchase the property on which the city hall stands, so that the company's facilities could expand. The resulting negative publicity took the company, and Cashmere, by surprise. Liberty Orchards defended its position that Cashmere, as the "Home of Aplets & Cotlets," would be much more successful than any other concept marketing that the town could use. However, the town's leadership and many citizens felt that the company had asked them to "sell out this town" (Egan 1997:1). Playing hardball, Liberty Orchards hinted at moving to nearby Leavenworth, a tourist destination with a Bavarian theme. A compromise of sorts was finally reached, and the town agreed to change a street name and the official slogan in order to retain its seventy-nine-year-old corporate citizen and major employer.

CORPORATE PHILANTHROPY AND COMMUNITY ECONOMIC DEVELOPMENT[1]

Another way of thinking about building a corporate concept marketing approach is to integrate corporate philanthropy into the development strategy. A shift in how corporations are viewing philanthropic activities holds particular relevance for community economic development efforts. The advent of "strategic philanthropy" is considered by some to be an outgrowth of hostile takeovers, downsizings, and leveraged buyouts that pervaded U.S. corporations in the late 1980s and into the 1990s. With budgets slashed, charitable giving was not a priority and "doing good for the sake of doing good" became less of a focus (Koch 1998). A new attitude towards giving by corporations has emerged from this era; while some call it "enlightened self-interest," others describe it as "sophisticated focused giving" (Sagawa et al. 1999). By focusing dollars on issues and causes that directly affect their business success, corporations are trying to use their donations to expand their markets and build good will simultaneously. Thus, strategic corporate philanthropy represents the "integration of contributions management into the overall strategic planning of the corporation" (Marx 1998). It holds particular relevance for those interested in utilizing corporate relations for community economic development purposes.

Strategic philanthropy can be defined as "corporate giving that serves a dual purpose of contributing needed funds to charitable causes while simultaneously benefiting the firm's financial bottom line and enhancing business political legitimacy" (Hemphill 1999). According to research by The Conference Board, corporations now strategically focus their donations to

1. support programs favored by their customers and shareholders;
2. provide more noncash support such as employee volunteer programs, products, and services; and
3. aggressively publicize their donations (Koch 1998).

The trend of strategic philanthropy is likely to continue as more corporations integrate this approach into their marketing and development efforts. Others argue that it is more than a trend, that it is absolutely essential for corporations to implement strategies and programs to develop trust within their communities (Burke 1999).

How can community economic development organizations benefit from this movement towards strategic philanthropy by corporations? Community economic development organizations are uniquely positioned within communities and regions to help corporations identify the most effective investments. As more corporations focus their donations into strategic philanthropy, the opportunity to form beneficial partnerships increases. The following summary reviews the process in various approaches of corporate strategic philanthropy programs—information that community economic development organizations can use to form philanthropic partnerships with corporations.

Corporate Philanthropy—Investing in the Community *and* the Business

From all indications, gone are the days when most corporations give purely for the sake of giving or because it is "the right thing to do." This shift from true philanthropy to donations as direct investments in the corporation's bottom-line is pervasive. Corporations now view contributions as spending shareholder equity, which requires them to justify these expenditures as investments that have "the strongest bottom-line impact to the business" (McKaughan 1995). While "self-interest" refers to the internal needs of a company, "enlightened self-interest" has been defined as what is good for the company *and* society (Ettorre1995).

This shift in how corporations determine, define, and make contributions has major implications. First, there is pressure on the corporate philanthropic staff to balance the need to answer to shareholders about expending their equity with investing in community projects that will both generate social good and increase corporate profitability (Himmelstein 1998). Each donation must be financially responsive to the corporation and the financial advantages of the donation must be clear—the more donations are viewed as investments, the more imperative it is to justify the expenditures. The vice president for corporate contributions for Johnson & Johnson Inc. explains that "Every donation made by a business has to have an acceptable explanation. With literally tens of thousands of contributions choices, a business must be able to explain why it singles out a specific nonprofit organization for support and how that decision fits in its overall contributions plan" (Weeden 1995).

Another implication is that the focus of giving is now much more narrow in terms of how the money is donated. Typically, corporations will have clear set priorities for giving in defined areas. For example, Citibank commits 80 percent of their contributions to two areas only, education and community development (Weeden 1995). Chrysler focuses its giving priorities from a general category of education to targeted job training (Marx 1998). What does this new narrow focus mean? Some proponents of this new way of giving believe that it is a win-win proposition, benefiting the corporation's profitability while helping communities address their issues and problems. A company tends to "throw the full weight of its resources, not just grant dollars" behind its focus, once a partner is identified (Koch 1998). This results in a targeted, intense approach to partnering.

In essence, the business and philanthropic divisions of corporations have merged their interests to develop strategies that can, as Craig Smith (1994:105) describes, "increase their name recognition among consumers, boost employee productivity, reduce R&D costs, overcome regulatory obstacles, and foster synergy among business unit . . . to give companies a powerful competitive edge."

Giving Until It Doesn't Hurt: Types of Programs

Several types of programs have emerged in this era of strategic philanthropy. While the programs vary according to corporate goals and priorities, some common themes underlie the approaches. Four types of programs—in-kind giving, corporate employee volunteer programs, venture philanthropy, and cause-related marketing—are summarized here.

In-Kind Giving

This type of giving entails non-monetary exchanges of services or products that are donated to other organizations. Somaya (1996:32) defines this type of activity from the corporate perspective as:

leveraging an activity that is integral to a business' operation to achieve some social gain, without incurring significantly different costs than the reasonable business alternatives available to that company . . . the corporation can utilize its various operating, financial, and intangible resources as part of its ongoing corporate strategy to have positive impact on its community's development.

The motivation for corporations to provide in-kind services and donated products includes the fact that, in some cases, companies can convert surplus inventory into valuable tax deductions. The value of the tax deductions is often worth twice as much as the cost of the service or product being donated (Reder 1995). Tax deductions are a powerful motivation, and the recipients of the surplus property also benefit. For example, numerous schools have received computer systems that are outdated for corporate purposes but sufficient to enhance learning for students.

Corporate Employee Volunteer Programs

Some companies have implemented comprehensive programs for their employees to donate time to community development activities. Kodak has just such a program and is very active in the communities where it is located (Ettorre 1995). Other companies, such as 3M and IBM, encourage their employees to donate their expertise, and support their efforts in the form of paid leaves of absence. Volunteerism, an alternative form of corporate giving, encourages employees to devote time and resources to specific nonprofit and government organizations. Many of the corporate volunteer programs focus on educational activities such as student mentoring and "adopting" local schools, for valid reason. The Conference Board found in an extensive study that those businesses with volunteer educational programs have discovered a competitive advantage in integrating learning as a vital organizational component at all levels (Murphy 1995). Not only do these programs benefit the overall corporate strategy for performance, they provide a human resource tool as well. Volunteer programs serve to attract and retain employees, build skills, and foster job satisfaction. The attraction of corporate volunteer programs affects profits in another way too: volunteer programs cost much less than professional development seminars and provide many of the same benefits (Murphy 1995).

Venture Philanthropy

Analogous in some respects to venture capital funds, "venture philanthropy" (Kosminsky 1997) funds are becoming more frequent. The sponsoring corporation provides the money, technical advice, and business expertise to community-based organizations for targeted activities. Similar to venture capital funds, the risks can be high as untested ideas often are funded; however, if successful, the rewards include creating new opportunities and wealth to address community problems (Kosminsky 1997).

For example, Pfizer created the Community Ventures Fund in 1995 to support local community economic development efforts. Grants support organizational development, business and marketing plan development, and infrastructure. The results are impressive thus far, with community-based organizations empowered and Pfizer meeting its goals of supporting community economic development activities through targeted giving.

Cause-Related Marketing

Philanthropy can be considered as a marketing technique for corporations. Unlike other forms of marketing, philanthropy holds the potential to generate benefits beyond selling more products, but may backfire if marketing efforts are not well received (Himmelstein 1998), or if the nonprofit or governmental partner feels that credibility is affected. More and more companies are willing to take this chance. A recent study indicated that cause-related marketing efforts and expenditures have increased significantly (File and Prince 1998).

Studies have indicated that the benefits to corporations of cause-related marketing are far reaching: Consumers are more likely to try a new brand as a result of cause related promotion, as well as remember the companies' advertisements (File and Prince 1998). Government and nonprofits benefit too, with more choices of funding sources and the potential to increase awareness of their missions.

There are numerous examples of cause-related marketing efforts. Reder (1995) illustrates several efforts:

- Ben and Jerry's Partnership Program helps match retail business opportunities with communities' social needs. For example, the company oversaw the development of an ice cream shop in Baltimore to be operated and owned by People Encouraging People, a nonprofit rehabilitation program for the disabled.
- Jantzen, a major swimwear manufacturer headquartered in Oregon, sponsor several beach cleanups per year along the coastline, promoting environmental awareness and brand name identity.
- Habitat for Humanity, a nonprofit organization focused on providing affordable housing, has benefited tremendously by forging a partnership with Home Depot, a logical ally.

Community Economic Development Organizations as a Natural Ally for Corporate Strategic Philanthropy

Community economic development organizations understand their regions and communities and can identify with and respond to local issues and opportunities most effectively. They represent an effective means for helping corporations accomplish their strategic philanthropy goals, especially when local development goals coincide with those priorities that corporations want to support. Additionally, community economic development organizations focus on making their communities good places to do business, often by lowering the costs of doing business and favorably affecting companies' profitability. Thus, community economic development organizations help companies increase their profitability while serving the community.

Working with the private sector to encourage growth and development within communities is the business of economic developers. Several strategies can be integrated into community economic development programs to fully realize the benefits of corporate strategic philanthropy:

- *Identify potential corporate partners.* Corporations in the community should be assessed for their level of involvement in corporate philanthropy. Are they currently participating in cause-related marketing, selected programs, or special events? Do their parent organizations have foundations or defined corporate giving programs? Corporations outside the community are potential partners— many regional, state, and national corporations have no geographic restrictions in providing funding.

- *Assess community needs and potential projects.* What nonprofit or public organizations exist in the community? What are their funding needs, project priorities, goals? Are there unmet needs in the community that could support community economic development—for example, worker training programs or educational enhancement? A list of "fundable" projects needs to be devised, then prioritized.

- *Target corporate foundations in fund-raising efforts.* Including potential corporate foundations in a fund raising strategy serves to broaden the community economic development organization's exposure and ability to achieve their goals. Thousands of corporate foundations in the United States support community, education, and community economic development-related projects. The key is to match the community's needs with the funding priorities of corporate foundations. Just as with targeted marketing efforts for industrial prospects, corporate foundations represent a potential investor in the community and should be approached accordingly.

- *Integrate corporate partners into the community economic development process.* What is it that corporations want to, or need to, achieve by participating in strategic philanthropy? If the economic developer can identify these needs and provide a venue for helping to achieve them, then a strategic alliance that benefits both partners will result.

Kosminsky (1997) included a quote from one of the recipients of Pfizer's 1997 venture philanthropy fund that sums up the relationship between community development organizations and corporate philanthropy very well: "Philanthropy provides tools—but it must be the community organization that puts those tools to work" (Kominsky 1997:30). Further, Kosminsky provides a summary of some of the characteristics that corporations are looking for in their nonprofit philanthropic partners when funding local community economic development activities:

- Community based, with local leadership
- A focus on individuals' needs and how to achieve success for those persons
- Emphasis on welcoming new businesses and capital
- Demonstrate an abiding faith in the abilities of people to decisively make positive differences. (Kosminsky 1997)

Just as organizations have marketed themselves to corporations for soliciting investments in the form of business locations, it is possible to market the community as a partner for philanthropic activities. Strategic philanthropy has firmly entered the corporate environment—now the time has come for it to become more a part of the community economic development lexicon.

CORPORATE CULTURE

In some cases, communities have aligned themselves (either deliberately or through dominant private-sector actions) with the identity of a corporation or its products. The resulting corporate iconicism serves as the basis for concept marketing approaches. The following three vignettes provide summaries of different methods for utilizing corporate relationships for a community's benefit. Austin, Minnesota's story is one of participatory approach, involving the nonprofit, public, and the private sectors. The Hormel Foods Company had been operating in Austin for 100 years when the effort to use SPAM as the basis for a concept marketing approach began to grow. Hershey, Pennsylvania, is the story of a corporate town, with a twist: the industrialist envisioned a complete community concept in the early 1900s that included entertainment and education. This is a story that was, and is, primarily driven by a dominant corporate force within a community. Newark, Ohio's concept marketing approach has been developed steadily over the last several decades by a cottage industry that grew to a multibillion dollar corporation. The efforts, and investments, of this corporation have been the driving force behind the increased volume of tourists visiting the area and have conferred benefits on several towns throughout the region. In both the latter two vignettes, private corporations are the primary force behind the concept marketing approach and the communities' public and nonprofit organizations use the corporate identities to help market their respective interests.

AUSTIN, MINNESOTA
POPULATION: 22,000
CONCEPT: SPAM TOWN, USA

Located in southeastern Minnesota just 12 miles north of the Iowa border, Austin is an example of a corporate town that has built on existing manufacturing activity to expand its appeal. In 1891, George Hormel established what is known today as Hormel Foods, a multinational meat and food processing agglomerate. In 1937, the company introduced the canned meat product SPAM. Despite derogatory remarks aimed at the product, it has gained an international reputation as an almost indestructible dietary staple. It seems to have permanently entered the psyche of Americans during World War II, when it was a staple in the diet of soldiers (Corbett 1995).

SPAM has provided more than job opportunities to citizens of Austin—it is the basis for a concept marketing approach that attracts national attention and scores of visitors.

Developing the Concept

George Hormel first arrived in Austin as a traveling salesman. He established a meat market and packing hop with a partner in 1887 (George A. Hormel & Co. 1991). Due to differences in how the partners viewed the operation, George Hormel assumed control of the packinghouse in 1891, and the rest is history. He explained his vision in a letter written to his mother: "I am sure of success at Austin, more so than I was in any enterprise. Now don't think I'm going to be just another butcher—that isn't what I am going into" (George A. Hormel & Co. 1991:15).

The company expanded dramatically and quickly entered the national markets, earning a solid reputation for quality processed meat products. Not only were national markets in George Hormel's sight, he expanded into international markets as early as 1905 (George A. Hormel & Co. 1991:200). World War I cut the international business short, and it was not until 1955 that international markets were again targeted for the company's products.

With World War II came the increasing popularity of SPAM, a canned meat product made from pork. Of the company's 1,600 products, SPAM remains the top seller. No one is really sure why, but most recognize the phenomenon. Hormel Foods states that Hawaiians eat more SPAM per person that any other U.S. residents, followed by Alaska, Texas, and Alabama (Corbett 1995:A5). Beginning in 1990, Hormel Foods began organizing and underwriting the costs of an annual SPAM festival, the "Spamjam." The festival has grown to attract numerous visitors—at the 2000 festival over 20,000 people representing forty-eight states and several other countries attended the one-day event (Harris 2001). It is part of a four-day SPAM Town USA Festival that is sponsored by the Austin Chamber of Commerce, the Austin Convention and Visitors Bureau, and the City of Austin.

SPAM Town USA, the basis of the concept marketing approach, was first initiated in 1997 as a combination of prior festivals. The name also became the official marketing slogan of the town, with the Austin City Council proclaiming their city SPAM Town, USA. With aggressive marketing, the festival has attracted even larger crowds and serves as the primary marketing effort for the area's tourism-based activities (Samuels 2001).

In addition to the festival, a small museum of 800 square feet provides visitors with insight into the development of SPAM as a cultural phenomenon. Even with the crowded quarters, the museum attracts over 60,000 visitors annually (Harris 2001).

Outcomes

In September of 2001, the new SPAM Museum opened. The 16,500-square-foot facility includes exhibits on the history of Hormel Foods and SPAM; an auditorium and theater; opportunities to don Hormel Foods uniforms and see the SPAM production line; a gift store; clips of historic commercials of SPAM; a World War II display depicting the role of SPAM as a food source for millions of soldiers; and an interactive SPAM exam (Austin Convention and Visitors Bureau 2001).

Yet, Hormel Foods has contributed more than SPAM to Austin. Originally established in 1942, the Hormel Institute has become one of the nation's leading centers for lipid research. The faculty and staff of biochemists, cellular and molecular biologists, nutritionists, and biophysicists conduct research for expanding knowledge of the role of lipids in health and disease (Austin Convention & Visitors Bureau 2000).

A charitable foundation was established by Hormel Foods to benefit the community. Over $7 million has been donated for public school renovations, and the corporation supports the public library, the YMCA, and other Austin institutions (Harris 2001). The company participates willingly with the Austin Chamber of Commerce and the city to formulate marketing plans for Austin that involve lending the SPAM registered trademark (and reputation) for promotional purposes (Forstner 2000).

HERSHEY, PENNSYLVANIA
POPULATION: 12,500
CONCEPT: CHOCOLATE TOWN, USA

Hershey is a household name that conjures up images of chocolate. But Milton Hershey, the product's inventor, had more than developing a great product on his mind: he envisioned a new town built around the factory. In 1903, the candy entrepreneur constructed a massive chocolate factory in his hometown of Derry Church, utilizing the supplies of milk from local dairy farms. By 1906, the township had renamed itself Hershey (Harrisburg-Hershey-Carlisle-Perry Co. Tourism and Convention Bureau 2000). Milton Hershey's vision of creating an enjoyable and pleasant town for the company's employees was realized and exceeded, to become a tourist destination. The company, now called Hershey Foods Corporation and headquartered in Milton Hershey's mansion, dominates the town, owning 42 percent of the real estate (Fox 1999).

Hershey is home to the largest chocolate manufacturing facility in the world. This is a story of a company town, and probably the most extensive successful development of a community by a corporation in the United States.

Developing the Concept

The concept began with Milton Hershey's vision. He orchestrated the construction of many facilities and amenities for his workers, including parks, schools, public buildings, and homes (Benini 1994). Each home had an individualized design and the avenues were named places where cocoa is grown.

Hershey's design included a campus, or park-like environment. Hershey Park, begun in 1907, grew to include a Dentzel carousel, a zoo, a baseball stadium, a midway, sunken gardens, a scenic railroad, bowling alleys, tennis courts, an amphitheater, and numerous other attractions that served the company's employees and citizens of Hershey (Coffey 1997). Located at the corner of Cocoa and Chocolate Avenues, the park served as a focal point for the community. By the mid 1920s, a Convention Hall was added, as well as a dancing pavilion and stage, hosting music celebrities such as Glenn Miller, Tommy Dorsey, and Louis Armstrong (Coffey 1997:17). In later years, the park has been developed into a theme park that draws visitors from all parts of the nation.

During the Great Depression, Milton Hershey hired workers to construct a Community Building and the palatial Hotel Hershey. Capitalizing on out-of-work laborers and dropping prices for construction materials, the project employed over 800 workers and was completed in 1933 (Hershey Foods Corporation 2000). The Hotel Hershey is a member of the Historic Hotels of America and is a considerable attraction. drawing visitors to Hershey.

As the number of visitors to Hershey increased, the company decided that the factory could no longer accommodate the high volume of requests for tours. In the 1970s, Chocolate World was created to provide free tours of the chocolate-making process (Clark 2000). A gift shop, food court, full-service restaurant, and information center complete the experience.

Outcomes

Chocolate World is the world's most visited corporate center, with nearly 3 million visitors per year (Clark 2000). This is more visitors than the White House in Washington, D.C. receives annually. Hershey's Chocolate World Visitors Center is the official information center for the Hershey Foods Corporation. The corporation maintains a Web site to supply information about visiting Hershey, similar to the type of marketing data that a chamber of commerce would provide. Developing the concept of Hershey has definitely been a private sector effort (via the Hershey Foods Corporation), although the chamber of commerce and the regional convention and visitors bureau use the Hershey name for their marketing purposes (Wagner 2001).

In 1971, the park began to be converted from a regional attraction to an amusement park that would draw a national audience. It is one of the "greenest" theme parks in the country, with lavish landscaping and a rolling terrain. By 1997, Hersheypark attracted 2.1 million visitors, ranking twenty-seventh in *Amusement Business*'s roster of North American theme parks (Amusement Business 1997). Additionally, the Hersheypark Stadium has consistently attracted large crowds with a variety of entertainment events. *Amusement Business* also rates stadiums, and Hersheypark rated first in the top fifteen stadiums in the nation with less than 40,000 capacity for two out of the three-year period, 1993–1996 (Powell 1996).

The park provides more than an employment opportunity for Hershey's citizens. It provides a sense of community as well. Many of the employees frequented the park as children and grew up to work for Hersheypark. The park was part of the process of realizing Milton Hershey's vision of community and avoiding the drabness of typical factory towns (Coffey 1997:15).

Milton Hershey's philanthropic activities benefited the citizens of Hershey in numerous ways. In 1909, he and his wife, Catherine, established a school for orphans. In 1918, he endowed the school with his entire holdings of Hershey Chocolate Company stock, worth $60 million (Golden 1999). In 1999, the school had amassed a $752 million surplus on the endowment which had grown to $5 billion—exceeding those of Stanford University and the Massachusetts Institute of Technology (Golden 1999:1). The school serves 1,100 students, from kindergarten through high school, mostly from single parent families. In 1935, Milton Hershey established a small, private charitable foundation for cultural and educational opportunities for local residents (Hershey Foods Corporation 2000). It supports the Hershey Museum Gardens, the Hershey Theatre and the Hershey Community Archives. Other philanthropic activities include the $50 million gift to establish the Pennsylvania State University Medical Center.

It is unusual for a corporate image to be so highly ingrained in a town's identity. Hershey is an exception, given the vision and dedication to the town by its creator, Milton Hershey. The entire town reflects his ideals for community life, and even the smell of chocolate permeates the air. Hershey is one of the best examples of how one person's vision, combined with a corporation's resources, can literally create a community and its environment.

NEWARK, OHIO
POPULATION: 48,950
CONCEPT: BASKET COUNTRY

Newark is home to The Longaberger Company's headquarters which is a free-standing, seven-story replica that is 160 times larger than the company's trademark product: a woven market basket with handles (see Photograph 3.1). This alone attracts numerous visitors to the city, but Newark cannot claim the cor-

Photograph 3.1
The Longaberger Company Headquarters, Newark, Ohio

porate relationship completely, as Longaberger has ties to the greater region. Nearby Frazeyburg and Dresden in the adjoining county are home to Longaberger facilities, and it is the village of Dresden that originally housed the company's retail basket stores. Thus, the concept of "basket country" really describes the greater Newark region in central Ohio.

Newark, named in 1802 for its counterpart in New Jersey, first attracted settlers because of the suitability of the area for farming and for the plentiful game (Newark and Licking County Chamber of Commerce 2000). The rolling hills provided scenic vistas and the area prospered with a diversified industrial base after the railroad arrived in the mid 1800s. The economy of Newark is almost equally divided between agriculture and miscellaneous industries. Licking County has over 100 manufacturing establishments and is the fourth largest agricultural producing county in the state (Newark and Licking County Chamber of Commerce 1997). In the 1990s, Newark and the surrounding area became increasingly identified with baskets produced by The Longaberger Company.

Developing the Concept

J. W. Longaberger started making hand-woven baskets with his father in 1919, in Dresden. He and his wife had twelve children, all of whom learned the family's basketmaking tradition. His fifth child, Dave, would carry the tradition to new heights. Dave Longaberger first started in business in Dresden by opening a restaurant in 1963, and then a grocery store. In 1972, he asked his father to make market baskets to sell, which quickly evolved into the idea for the new J. W.'s Handwoven Baskets Company, established a year later (Shipley 2000) as a cottage industry.

The enterprise grew and was renamed The Longaberger Company. Manufacturing facilities were built, and by 2000, the company had $850 million in sales, 7,600 employees, and 60,000 sales associates. As the largest manufacturer of hand-woven baskets in the United States, The Longaberger Company has added several venues to expand its market appeal as a destination site, such as a golf course, a hotel, and an entertainment park. The funding for all the facilities has been provided by the company. The effort to develop the concept therefore has been a private sector initiative. However, the area's chamber of commerce and the convention and visitors bureau have used the increasing popularity of the company's products and venues for marketing efforts. The company's headquarters building is featured in marketing publications, including the cover of a CD-Rom sent to prospective visitors. Tourism has increasingly become more important to the region, and the Longaberger facilities are a major draw, including the Longaberger shops and facilities in Dresden, and the headquarters building in Newark.

Outcomes

The Longaberger Experience is a road trip along Route 16 from Newark to Dresden that provides several venues for tourists. In Newark, the unusual architecture of the company headquarters building draws thousands annually. Dave Longaberger conceived of the idea to symbolize the heritage of the company (J. Pearce 2000). The 180,000-square-foot facility houses 500 employees and incorporates a 30,000-square-foot atrium, a 142-seat auditorium, and two handles that weigh 150 tons. Costing $30 million to construct, the building has been described as a gigantic billboard, a piece of pop art, and a brilliant exercise in corporate advertising (The Longaberger Company 2000). This monument to a company that built its business on baskets provides both a site for operating the company as well as an attraction for visitors (Quintanilla 1997). Other facilities in Newark include The Place Off the Square, a 117-room downtown hotel, as well as two theaters funded by The Longaberger Company.

The next stop in the tour is the Longaberger Golf Club, along Route 16. Designed by a nationally renowned architect, the facility is a seventy-two par, eighteen hole public course and a participant in the Audubon International Signature Cooperative Sanctuary Program. Further along the route is the manufacturing campus at Frazeysburg. It consists of numerous facilities for producing the company's products, and offers tours for the public. Adjacent to the campus is The Longaberger Homestead, consisting of seven buildings offering educational demonstrations, as well as shopping and other activities. An historic barn was relocated to the site to provide a venue for performances, a basketmaking shop, and restaurants. A replica of the family home and J. W. Longaberger's original workshop are also included.

The village of Dresden, population 1,600, is the final stop on the road trip. Popeye's Soda Shop—Dave's restaurant first opened in 1963—is operated by the company as well as several specialty shops. Other shops, not owned by The Longaberger Company attract visitors to the village too. Because Dresden is the hometown of the Longaberger family, the company has strong ties and is committed to the community. The Longaberger Foundation was established in 1999, the year Dave Longaberger passed away, with his daughter as president (his eldest daughter had assumed the position of president of The Longaberger Company in 1994). The company has been a generous benefactor to Dresden and the region, providing facilities such as a senior center and a swim and fitness center.

If not careful, companies can overpower a community and alienate the citizens and civic leaders. The Longaberger Company, however, has been a valuable and generous corporate citizen. *Inc.* magazine named Dave Longaberger one of the top socially responsible entrepreneurs in the year 1992. *Working Mother* magazine named the company one of the 100 Best Companies for Working Mothers in 1998, citing their day-care facility and high percentage of women managers. *George* magazine gave it an honorable mention as one of the most generous companies in the United States in 1999, for its 24-hour on-site health care center provided free of charge to its employees, and its $9 million in donations to charity from 1996 to 1999.

SUMMARY

Linking a community's identity with a corporation, or one of its brand names, can be tremendously beneficial. There are several considerations for developing a concept marketing approach based on corporate iconicism that a community needs to investigate before starting the development process. These include:

1. Is a corporation located within the community or region that may serve as a partner in developing a concept marketing approach?

2. What level of participation would the corporation be willing to help with the concept development?

    a. Lending identity via a brand product

    b. Developing a corporate tour or museum venue

    c. Cooperating with the nonprofit and public sectors in a development partnership

    d. Promoting the area via marketing activities

    e. Direct funding to support community-based marketing and development activities

3. If there is not a corporation in the area to partner in concept marketing development, are there smaller companies that could participate jointly to promote a product identify for the area?

4. What is the level of corporate citizenship in the community already? This may indicate the logical partners or approach to take.

5. Is there active corporate philanthropy in the community? If not, are there other sources for partnering with corporations for philanthropic purposes?

The last consideration, regarding corporate philanthropy, is vital in a community's effort to develop a corporate concept marketing approach. Economic development organizations are uniquely positioned within communities and regions to help corporations identify their most effective philanthropic investments (R. Phillips 2000a). As more corporations transmute their donations into strategic philanthropy, the opportunity to form beneficial partnerships increases. It is worth investigating so that valuable relationships are not overlooked.

Concept marketing based on corporate iconicism is not without risk. Some communities may find that there is inadequate support from either the corporate entity or the public to form the basis for the marketing approach. In the case of Austin, Minnesota, both the company and the civic sector had to overcome the negative stigmatism associated with the union strike against Hormel Foods in 1985. Lasting over a year and a half, the strike threatened to tear apart the community, and violence escalated until National Guard troops were called in to quell the discord. With time, the community has healed and Hormel Foods is once again perceived as a benevolent and beneficial partner. In 1997, the city and the company partnered to expand its corporate identity, with the SPAM Town USA concept marketing campaign, which has achieved its mission of increasing tourism and related activities in Austin.

The allure of a potentially dramatic increase in tourism to corporate-sponsored venues can create too heavy a reliance on one economic element in a community. The relationship with the corporate entity literally dictates the outcomes for the community; if the corporation suffers a major decline, the community suffers as well. Worse, if the image of the corporation receives negative publicity, the community's linked image experiences negativity, too.

A community must ask itself if it is willing to give up some degree of autonomy, depending on the level of dominance of the corporate entity. A community may find that it has lost decision-making power, if the corporation dictates the outcomes. Conversely, if the corporation is a truly benevolent partner with the community's best interests as a motivating goal, the community can reap benefits otherwise unobtainable. A community using corporate iconicism as the basis for building a concept marketing approach must address these issues and balance the needs of the community with the potential trade-offs and benefits of linking to a corporate identity.

NOTE

1. This section has been excerpted with permission from an article by Rhonda Phillips, "Using Corporate Strategic Philanthropy for Economic Development," *Economic Development Review* 17, no. 1 (August 2000): 7–11.

4

Retail-Based Development for Structuring the Concept

Retail as a community economic development strategy?! Although retail has not been traditionally considered a major economic development component of communities development plans, many communities have begun to consider seriously retail in this regard. Some communities find that encouraging retail development, including targeting retail establishments for recruitment into the area, results in many positive benefits. In communities that are not able to sustain or attract manufacturing or other types of revenue-building and employment activities, retail can serve as a viable alternative to stabilize and enhance local economies.

OUTLETS AND MALLS AS DEVELOPMENT STRATEGY

Some communities have built their concept marketing strategy as a retail destination—manufacturers' discount outlet "towns" illustrate this approach. Auburn, Washington, a town of less than 40,000 knows the impact of outlet retailing intimately: they are home to the SuperMall, the Northwestern United State's largest outlet mall. With 1.2 million square feet of retail space that includes a 185,000 square foot electronics amusement park, the mall draws over 7 million visitors per year (Szymanksi 1996). This further impacts the community with supporting development, such as hotel and restaurants. Prior to its development, over 75 percent of Auburn residents shopped outside the city limits (Wolcott 1994); now, an estimated $3,000,000 in additional sales tax revenues flow to the community. With over 4,000 jobs added because of the SuperMall, the economic development impact of this community's retail-based strategy has been dramatic.

Other communities, such as North Conway, New Hampshire, see outlets as a supplement to their primary economic activity. In this case, tourism and recreation is the primary contributor to the economy, and the development of a large outlet mall in the city is seen as a supplement to capture additional tourist dollars. San Marcos, Texas, is another example where outlet retail shopping is seen as a supplement to a diversified economic development strategy. San Marcos has created reinvestment zones, a foreign trade zone, a revolving loan fund, the Main Street Program, and a tax and development fee abatement programs (Fletcher 1993). Outlet shopping is only one of the attractions that the city promotes. Some communities have inherited outlets as an economic activity, such as the case with Secaucus, New Jersey. The public sector did not feel the need to get involved, and let the private corporations manage Secaucus's emergence as a "famous outlet city" (Constantino 2000). Many large distribution warehouses are located in Secaucus because of its close proximity to New York City; the owners decided to sell merchandise directly from the warehouses. Real estate developers seized upon the idea of Secaucus as a retail center and developed outlet and strip malls to further develop the area.

In addition to outlet malls, other types of mall development are being used to bolster community's economies too. Upscale mall development that includes entertainment is emerging as one of the newer approaches. Many urban and suburban areas are pursuing this type of development; however, it also holds applicability to small and mid-sized communities as well. Roseville, California, with a population of 74,000, entered a public-private partnership to develop the 1.1 million-square-foot super-regional mall. The City of Roseville provided approximately $20 million in infrastructure support for the project—streets, and water and sewer lines—with the expectation that much more sales and property tax revenues will be generated (Walter 1997). The design of this new generation mall is unusual, with Greek Revival arches and columns, dramatic colors, and an outdoor pedestrian streetscape to pull together restaurants and ancillary retailers that often are located on the outskirts of a mall property (Johnson 2000).

However, Roseville has taken retail-based development a step further: they not only partnered to bring in the super regional upscale mall, they have for many years invested in their downtown district for retail expansion and preservation. The city has invested in new streetscapes and utilities, as well as downtown redevelopment programs such as the Façade Renovation Program, loans for business development, and a fee deferment program (Garner 2000). In the late 1980s, the city partnered with private sector interests to create an Auto Mall located downtown to stimulate activity. This successful effort has helped foster a vibrant downtown economy for Roseville.

DOWNTOWN REVITALIZATION AND THE ROLE OF RETAIL

A development strategy based on retail is not a new concept. The National Trust for Historic Preservation's Main Street Program is devoted to the strategy of reinvigorating traditional and historic downtowns and neighborhood commercial districts across the United States. Combined with preservation and rehabilitation of historically significant architecture, the Main Street Program focuses on the rebirth of vibrant downtowns, with retail as a major component. From tiny Bonaparte, Iowa (population 500), to Saratoga Springs, New York, to the East Carson district of Pittsburgh's South Side, the Main Street Program has been implemented as a public-private alliance for community redevelopment (National Main Street Center 1996). Working with over 1,600 communities since 1980, the Main Street Program has garnered over $15 billion in public and private reinvestments in these communities, generating over 52,000 new businesses and 200,000 new jobs (Main Street Program 2001a:2). One measure used to evaluate Main Street Program's successes in communities is the reinvestment ratio, which is the average number of dollars generated in each community for every dollar used to operate the local Main Street Program. At $39.22 dollars reinvested for every $1 spent on local Main Street Program's revitalization efforts (Main Street Program 2001a:2), it generates a great return.

Each year, the National Trust for Historic Preservation recognizes exceptional accomplishments in revitalizing historic and traditional downtowns and neighborhood commercial districts. In 2001, the following five communities were winners of the Great American Main Street Award. Each of these communities exhibits innovation and perseverance for creating their own redevelopment concepts. A brief summary of their accomplishments is listed below (Main Street Program 2001b:1–2):

- Danville, Kentucky: This community built its concept on the basis of always being "first": the first post office west of the Allegheny Mountains, the first courthouse in Kentucky, and other notable occurrences. The City of Firsts decided to resist sprawl and focus on revitalizing downtown with small business incentives and investments in infrastructure.

- Elkader, Iowa: This once dying small town ravaged by declines in agriculture staged its own funeral procession, which rallied the community to save itself from further economic decline. Not able to compete with the "big box" retailers of nearby cities, Elkader focuses on heritage tourism and historic preservation to save its economy.

- Mansfield, Ohio: When a mall opened in this community, downtown businesses closed and buildings were left vacant. Not satisfied with the imminent demise of its downtown, Mansfield community leaders built an old-fashioned carousel in its heart and spurred its rebirth.

- Enid, Oklahoma: As with Mansfield, Enid's downtown declined rapidly after a mall opened. In response, a redevelopment plan was formulated, including conversion of a grocery warehouse into a learning center and the development of a 1920s style downtown ballpark.

THEMING RETAIL

Some communities develop a theme concept, such as a destination for antiquing or specialty products. Examples include Marshal, Texas, noted as the "pottery capital of the world." Many of these communities formed their retail-based concepts by default: a company in the community is noted for production or distribution of specialty products. This is the case of Springfield, Missouri, noted as the Bass Pro Shops sporting goods retail mecca for the outdoor enthusiast. This major retail attraction brings 3.5 million visitors annually. Communities can build on the presence of these specialty products retailers to broaden the appeal of their area, such as promoting the recreational opportunities of the Springfield region to attract the shoppers at Bass Pro Shops. Indeed, the Springfield Web site promotes the area as being within a "100-mile radius of more than 7,500 miles of shoreline, along with accessible lakes, floatable streams and rivers. Excellent hunting, camping and fishing are found throughout the area, amidst rolling hills and clear spring-fed streams" (Springfield Missouri Chamber of Commerce 2000). This concept for Springfield has been inherited, in the sense that explicit efforts were not made to develop a marketing approach based on retail; rather, it has evolved due to the presence of a major company with specialty products.

Antiquing as a themed retail approach can be quite successful as well. Some communities are finding that underutilized historic structures can be converted into antique "malls"—large buildings that are subdivided to a number of antique dealers. Putnam, Connecticut (population 9,031), has used this approach very well. In the early 1990s, someone opened an antique store in the vacant area of downtown. Then another antique dealer subdivided an old department store into over 100 different areas for leasing by other dealers. The concept took off, and over 50 percent of the retail activity in Putnam is now antiques (Rovero 2000). The city quickly began to offer $5000 grants for improvements in the downtown district (Rovero 2000:2). They also invested in sidewalk and streetscape improvements, public facilities, and parking areas to accommodate the influx of shoppers.

Before individual cases are illustrated, background information is useful to understand the dimensions of retail development. The following section provides a review of the types of retail-based development and its importance as a community-based strategy.

THE CONTEXT: RETAIL AS DEVELOPMENT[1]

From a community development perspective, retail-based development is an often overlooked but vital component of local economies. Certainly the arguments for supporting retail-based development include the following:

- Retail is a "clean" development. Retail, in general, is considered to be less destructive to the natural environment in comparison with other land uses such as manufacturing. It is rarely opposed by citizen or environmental groups on the basis of possible environmental degradation (Brammer and Tomasik 1995).
- Retail is a growth industry. While employment has declined in manufacturing and other sectors, the retail sector continues to expand. Because retail follows population, retail businesses can significantly precede office and industrial development.

- Retail is a mainstay of local economies. Retail sales taxes are a major source of revenue for many communities. Additionally property taxes for retail-based developments generate income (Lackey and Eckenstahler 1995).

- On average, retail "returns" to the community, in the form of tax payments, are higher than office, residential, or industrial properties.

While some community leaders realize that retail can be a valuable component of community development strategies, others may not think of retail as "economic development." Lackey and Eckenstahler (1995:85) describe the situation very well with the following:

If you ask a room full of economic developers who their clients and prospects are, 100 percent would identify manufacturers. Many would talk about distribution facilities. Several would even discuss back office and corporate headquarters facilities. Few, if any, would talk about retail . . . yet each of their local economies may be losing tens of millions of dollars and thousands of jobs annual from lost retail sales—dollars being spent by the residents of their communities, outside those communities. If so much is at stake, why don't economic developers better understand their retail economies?

One of the reasons is that retail has historically been an "assumed" activity; that is, if manufacturing, distribution, and other "industrial" investments flow to a community, retail will follow. However, retail can be just as powerful a community investment, particularly if the retail-based development is an attraction for a regional area. The litmus test for when to count retail as economic development is this:

If the retail development increases the amount of income available in a community by bringing in outside expenditures, and helps to reduce retail expenditure leakage from the community, then it is considered as vital as traditional industrial activities. (Pittman and Phillips 1995)

Outlet Centers

National consumer products companies increasingly sell directly to the consumer. The stores are attractive to both value-seeking consumers and manufacturers (Boling 1995:89). One of the most lucrative methods for manufacturers to reduce overproduction is through outlet centers. The centers are often located on interstate highways to attract passing traffic. Even smaller communities can capture outside retail expenditures for their local economies. Boaz and Foley, Alabama, and Stroud, Oklahoma, increased their sales tax revenues 200 percent the first year a Tanger outlet center opened in the town (Meyers 1995).

Some communities have recruited outlet stores into rehabilitated historic structures. For example, the town of Martinsburg, West Virginia, used old mill buildings to construct an outlet mall; downtown Durango, Colorado, converted historic storefronts for new street-level outlet shopping; and Freeport and Kittery, Maine, adapted houses and storefronts for an outlet district (Meyers 1995:54). The number of outlet stores and outlet centers in the United States increased dramatically in the 1980s, with moderate growth into the early 1990s (Gruen 1994). With creative conversions and mixed-use concepts now permeating how outlet shopping is developed, interest in outlet stores is likely to continue, even though the initial rush to build outlet malls has leveled off. Also, even urban areas that were not considered viable locations for outlet shopping are incorporating outlet stores into their retail mix: Chattanooga, Tennessee's famous Warehouse Row utilizes former railroad warehouses for outlet stores; and a Chicago suburbs has gotten on the bandwagon too, with an old piano factory converted into an outlet mall (Meyers 1995:54).

Regional Malls

Expenditures from outside the immediate community boundaries are attracted to regional malls that typically feature two or more major department store anchors (Casazza 1985). Usually in excess of 500,000 square feet, regional malls serve market areas that span 75 miles or more, particularly in those trade areas encompassing rural areas (Pittman and Phillips 1995:5–6). An emerging issue for regional malls, as well as for other types of retail-based development, is Internet-based competition. Some malls respond with improved layout and redesign to facilitate shopping—for example, clustering all related stores in one wing (Coleman 2000). Regional malls and the newer "mega malls," or super-regional facilities such as the Mall of America, can incorporate vast quantities of retail square footage, as well as inclusion of other functions such as community meeting spaces. These massive facilities are powerful economic contributors to host communities.

Community Centers

Community centers are smaller than regional malls, typically 150,000 to 300,000 square feet and usually include a junior or discount department store. "Power" centers containing stores such as Toys R Us draw in customers from outside the immediate community. Larger power centers may be as large as malls, with up to 1 million square feet and serve as new and redevelopment projects for regional customer draw (O'Mara et al. 1996).

However, in more densely populated urban areas, smaller community centers may serve only local customers and not draw in outside expenditures. Even if the community center is classified as a power center, some shopping centers are enjoying resurgence in popularity by market repositioning through design, renovation, or expansion (Schwanke et àl. 1994). By serving the varying needs of customers as areas change, these community centers contribute to a vital local economy. Market repositioning is welcomed by the host community as a strategy that avoids vacancies and decreased tax revenue flows.

Local Specialty Stores

In some cases, local specialty stores can reduce retail leakages from a community when customers purchase specialty products in other locales (Pittman and Phillips 1995). However, community economic developers can facilitate the development of local specialty stores to capture income that would otherwise be spent in different communities.

National Specialty Stores and Restaurants

Sometimes, customers leave a local economy to visit national retail chains, such as PepBoys auto supplies, Old Navy clothing, or PayLess Shoes; or national chain restaurants such as Red Lobster. Small to medium-sized communities can help offset this retail leakage by recruiting these types of retail-based developments when feasible.

Tourism and Entertainment-Based Retail Development

Communities can capitalize on clusters of specialty retail stores to draw in tourists. In some areas, specialty retail stores become the major tourist attraction. Restored historic retail districts, clustering of antique stores, and other types of specialty retail can be a powerful economic development strategy for some communities. For example, a developer in San Antonio, Texas, constructed a shopping center utilizing an old quarry and rock-crushing facility. The formerly abandoned industrial site that was an eyesore is now an economic engine, contributing tax revenues to the public treasury.

The internationally renowned River Walk in San Antonio further illustrates the power of combining unique design with retail and entertainment activities. Serving as one the largest tourist attractions in the state of Texas, the River Walk represents an amazing transformation from an area designed primarily for flood control of the San Antonio River to a pedestrian district that has few parallels in the nation. In the 1960s, local leaders decided to develop the area on each side of the river into a mecca for restaurants, retail establishments, entertainment activities, and hotels (Seel 2000). In addition to myriad independent specialty retail shops, a large mall has been built and integrated carefully into the River Walk design. The design of the River Walk is key to its success: it flawlessly integrated public works (drainage, flood control, and transportation infrastructure), historic preservation and architectural integrity of the buildings, public space and recreational opportunities, with retail and other commercial activities. It is, without doubt, one of the most successful examples of the public sector partnering with the private sector businesses to foster successful community revitalization.

Ybor City, a National Historic Landmark District located in Tampa, Florida, further illustrates how retail can be a vital component for both revitalization and tourism-based development. Ybor City is noted as the former Cigar Capital of the

World. Retail activities play a major and vital role in the district's economic revitalization, with plans announced recently for a major retail complex to be built in the middle of the district. The character of the area is extremely important, and the planning agency is striving to ensure architectural integrity of new construction with design and zoning standards. Urban renewal in the 1960s was ill fated, and in the late 1970s, the abandoned Hav-A-Tampa cigar factory was renovated as an ethnic mall complex. Other historic properties were rehabilitated, including a museum of the cigar industry. With this, Ybor City began its economic turnaround and is today a vibrant, exciting community incorporating entertainment, specialty retail, and a rich heritage. With the 1988 Ybor City Redevelopment Plan, the corporation ensured that zoning and other land use policies were supportive and flexible enough to encourage more retail-based development. The area's leadership recognized the importance of retail to the community's redevelopment efforts. Maricela Medrano, an urban planner with the Ybor City Development Corporation, explains the focus on retail: "We use retail as a major basis to create a friendly pedestrian environment and to reuse the historic structures with a use that is compatible with the size and scale of the streetscape" (Medrano 2000).

Since 1998, Ybor City has experienced an explosion in growth, both retail and mixed-use, incorporating high-density residential, office, and entertainment complexes. The area's tax base has increased to $33 million, providing revenues for reinvestment into the district through infrastructure improvements. These improvements and incentives, aimed at encouraging redevelopment of the historic properties (and when compatible with the land use plan, new construction) include: a tax increment financing district, transportation impact fee waivers, on-site storm water retention waivers, federal preservation tax credits assistance, Enterprise Zone tax credit assistance, ten-year ad valorem tax exemption, façade improvement loans, and U.S. Small Business Administration loan packaging services (Ybor City Development Corporation 2000). A joint venture is funding a $12 million parking structure and the regional transit authority and the City of Tampa are implementing a fixed-rail electric streetcar line linking Ybor City to two other districts in Tampa, for a total development cost of $23 million. Additionally, a $1.8 million infrastructure program is in progress, funded through the City of Tampa and the U.S. Economic Development Administration. Improvements, all of which will serve to support retail-based development, include a streetscaping project, construction of a gateway as a symbol for identifying Ybor City, and a district signage program to route pedestrian and vehicular traffic.

These incentives and improvements, coupled with the strong draw of the exciting cultural attributes of Ybor City have resulted in impressive gains in a formerly declining urban center: 180 new businesses operating in the district and 2000 new jobs. Over $115 million in project developments are in progress. Many of these focus on retail, such as the Centro Ybor project—a renovation of the historic Centro Espanol Building for a 210,000 square foot retail entertainment project (Ybor.org 2000). The complex includes a twenty-screen theater; total project cost is $45 million. Recently opened nearby is a $33 million mixed-use project with 462 apartment units and 10,000 square feet of retail space. The end result is the ongoing revitalization of an exciting district.

A newer version of tourism-related specialty stores is the urban entertainment district, that combines retail with other activities for a downtown experience. These may or may not include elements of festival marketplace development, such as that for the Inner Harbor of Baltimore, the San Antonio River Walk, or Underground Atlanta projects. Described as the hottest concept in retail, urban entertainment districts revitalize the economies of downtowns and suburban shopping areas (Beyard et al. 1998). The idea of using retail for entertainment has been reformulated to include exciting themes and aspects such as multimedia interaction, dramatic architectural design, games, and sports to provide innovative shopping experiences (Pegler 1998). A typology of entertainment-based retail development include: high-impact film venues (e.g., Imax combined with retail such as River-Center in New Orleans); entertainment-driven retail (e.g., CityWalk at Universal Studios in Los Angeles); brand-name retailing (e.g., Nike Town, Disney and Warner Brothers' stores); high-tech entertainment centers; and family entertainment centers such as Discovery Zone (P. Phillips 1995:14–15). The result is exciting destination shopping venues that add value to the consumers' experience through entertainment.

As illustrated, retail-based development strategies range widely. From encouraging small specialty shops for traditional downtown revitalization, to urban commercial district redevelopment, strategies can favorably impact economic development outcomes.

APPLICATIONS USING THE OUTLETS

Some communities have excelled at building strong retail outlet activities as a destination. The approach has varied, from explicit recruitment of manufacturers' outlets to inheriting the concept by default of the location of an outlet mall. Either way, the communities of Boaz, Alabama, and Manchester, Vermont, illustrate successful concept marketing strategies based on retail activities. Boaz's approach is to develop the town completely as an outlet retail destination. Manchester's approach is very different: they did not intentionally seek outlet retail, but when it started developing in the area, they made the most of it. Manchester was already an elegant resort village; coupling this with high-end retail outlet shopping has yielded a successful marketing concept.

BOAZ, ALABAMA
POPULATION: 8,300
CONCEPT: SHOPPER'S PARADISE

Timber and other natural resources such as abundant wild game and rich soil were the reasons that forty-seven people from Georgia settled in the Sand Mountain Plateau in 1878 (Boaz Chamber of Commerce 2001). The plentiful Southern

Pine trees in the area provided lumber for building homes and other structures. It was not until 1897 that the town was named Boaz, after a biblical character in the Book of Ruth. The early settlers engaged in agriculture as the primary economic activity, growing produce and milling sugarcane and sorghum for syrup. Related agricultural activities, such as cotton ginning, became the first significant industrial enterprise in the area. The town grew and became a small regional center, serving the agricultural hinterland of the Sand Mountain area. In the twentieth century, apparel manufacturing firms located in the area to take advantage of low-wage labor.

The location of the apparel manufacturers led to the concept of Boaz as a "shopper's paradise." A small town of 8,300 in the rolling hills of northern Alabama, Boaz is not located on an interstate highway, nor is it very close to an urban center. Despite the seemingly inconvenient and incongruent location, Boaz has recreated itself as a major retail-shopping destination. Its reliance on agriculture as its main economic activity has long passed, and retail is now the engine of the local economy (Riddle 2000).

The Impetus for Change

The effort to develop Boaz as a retail shopper's destination began in 1982, when over half of the downtown properties—many of them historic structures built in the late nineteenth century and early twentieth century—were vacant. The apparel manufacturers that had spurred growth early the twentieth century were closing or downsizing. As more local manufacturing plants began to close, the economic prospects for Boaz dimmed. Tax revenues stood at $665,000 and declining (Smith 2000).

The owners of the vacant Lee jeans factory on the edge of Main Street commercial district, the Vanity Fair Corporation, decided to convert the factory into a retail outlet for selling its merchandise. The project was immediately successful (Cain 1990) and the community leaders of Boaz had a new direction for revitalizing the economy—retail-based economic growth.

Developing the Concept

Because of the success of the Vanity Fair outlet in a defunct manufacturing facility, the community's leadership developed a strategy that departed dramatically from the conventional economic development approach of the time: instead of promoting the area to manufacturers and hoping to entice one to establish operations, they focused on recruiting retail-based outlet stores. Boaz gambled that this new and innovative strategy would pay off in the long term to help stabilize and revitalize the area's declining economy. Many small and mid-sized towns and cities spend most of their economic development budgets on promoting their areas to industrial prospects—firms that are willing to relocate or expand operations to a new site. Conventional wisdom among economic development professionals indicates that, on average, about 1,500 corporate expansions or relocations occur in the United States each year. Conversely, there are at least 15,000 economic development organizations in the United States; thus, the odds are not promising that most cities and towns will not secure a corporate expansion or relocation. The leaders of Boaz realized this and decided to take a radical departure from the conventional economic development approach of recruiting industrial prospects.

When Vanity Fair, a manufacturer in town, expressed its interest in setting up an outlet retail store, vigorous efforts began to draft a redevelopment strategy based on retail investment recruitment. Thus, Boaz became one of the first communities in the United States to develop an economic development recruitment strategy aimed at retailers, rather than manufacturers or distributors. The concept of an outlet town helped start a trend throughout the country of establishing outlet retail destinations.

The effort involved all three sectors, the public (City of Boaz), the private (business owners), and the nonprofit (the Boaz Chamber of Commerce). A contingency of leaders went to New York and other retail centers to recruit outlet stores to Boaz. The efforts to recruit factory outlets for the first couple of years were met with skepticism by retail executives (Cain 1990) who wondered why they would locate in a remote small town in Alabama. In 1984, three local businessmen decided to build the Boaz Outlet Center, with eight stores. This project was highly successful and more space was quickly added. After this, retail executives paid attention to Boaz and began opening a wide array of factory outlets.

An interesting note is that Boaz deliberately decided to recruit factory outlets to occupy its historic downtown structures. Rather than just build new malls on the outskirts of town, they wanted to incorporate downtown into its revitalization efforts. Additionally, Boaz realized early on that supporting infrastructure was key to the success of the concept. The City of Boaz invested in parking facilities for buses and cars, streetscaping, and other public facilities. The chamber of commerce developed festivals and other events to draw people, further increasing the flow of shoppers through Boaz. The private sector responded with development of hotels and restaurants to support shoppers' needs.

Outcomes

At the time Boaz started developing its marketing concept as an outlet destination, sales tax revenues were $600,000. By 1996, over 140 outlet stores were located in Boaz. Downtown had 100 percent occupancy, in its renovated historic buildings and new developments. Because downtown was at capacity, four more outlet malls or strips were developed adjacent to the area. Some adjustment has occurred in the last year in this mix, with a few downtown stores moving to the malls. Still, by 1996 there were over 140 outlet stores in Boaz, with over $4 million collected each year in sales tax revenues, most of which is generated by outlet sales.

Since 2000, Boaz has experienced a decline in retail sales and the number of outlets has fallen to around ninety (Maltbie 2000). Tax revenues fell to $3.6 million in 2000 (Walden 2000). The reason? As more towns and cities took note of Boaz's success as an outlet center, the strategy of recruiting outlets literally exploded in the 1990s. The result of this has been the development of many outlet centers throughout Alabama and the United States. With increased competition, it has been difficult for Boaz to maintain its stature as a premier outlet destination in the Southeast. Indeed, the astounding growth of outlet centers in the United States during the 1980s and 1990s overbuilt the market in some areas.

One of the responses to increased competition has been further investment in marketing activities to sell Boaz to new and returning shoppers. Originally, each outlet center conducted their own marketing efforts. Now, a council has been formed with members from the City of Boaz, each outlet center, and the Boaz Chamber of Commerce. ShopBoaz.com, an Internet-based marketing site, and other activities are used to promote interest in Boaz.

The impact of this development strategy has been impressive for Boaz. Charles Smith, the former Mayor of Boaz, summarizes the impact: "Retail shopping, especially connected to outlet store shopping, is a case where sales tax is the major contributor to local government budgets. Our property taxes are low, so we depend on this revenue stream that has been a boom for Boaz" (C. Smith 2000).

The city has used the increase in revenues to enhance its schools, build better transportation infrastructure, increase the level and quality of services, and improve streetscaping. Boaz has also attracted other investors to help diversify its economy. On average, the city expends about 10 percent of its sales tax revenues for improvements to support its retail-based developments. This return on investment is excellent.

In 2000, the Boaz outlet shopping complex ranked 15th in the nation in terms of its quality and ability to attract destination shoppers. On an average weekend day, over 2,000 people visit to shop. During special events, such as seasonal festivals, the number of tourists will increase to 50,000–80,000. Boaz experiences an incredible economic impact from over 300,000 visitors per year. The combination of utilizing renovated downtown buildings in a traditional small town setting and new adjacent construction with collaborative community leadership focused on retail-based development has been a highly successful strategy for Boaz.

MANCHESTER, VERMONT
POPULATION: 4,300
CONCEPT: RESORT SHOPPING

Few places have changed as rapidly as Manchester over the last several decades, leading one observer to dub it the "Land of Milk and Armani" (Coy 1993), in reference to the myriad designer outlets that have cropped up in the area. Although small in population and land size, Manchester has faced "big city" development pressures, especially in regard to land use decisions. It has responded in a manner that sets it apart from many other communities, which has resulted in the preservation of its unique character and tradition while promoting economic growth.

For over 200 years, Manchester has enjoyed a reputation as an up-scale resort community, with steep mountains enclosing the valley both east and west. The eighteenth-century Equinox Hotel still serves as the centerpiece of this elegant village. The Equinox is a white-columned, tower-topped resort with 180 rooms. Its appeal has endured throughout the centuries, attracting famous guests such as Presidents Taft, Theodore Roosevelt, Benjamin Harrison, and Grant (Krohn 2001). Abraham Lincoln's son adopted the village and built his summer home, Hildene, in Manchester. Other opulent and elegant mansions and cottages were constructed throughout the nineteenth century.

Supporting infrastructure for the grand resort village was developed during this time too: the Dorset Playhouse and the Weston Playhouse, the oldest summer theaters in the state, and the Southern Vermont Art Center, the state's oldest cultural institution in the state (Krohn 2001). This picturesque village is located at the base of Mount Equinox with its 3,800 foot peak right behind its namesake hotel. The lovely setting continues to draw numerous tourists.

Impetus for Change

Manchester did not actively seek to become an outlet mecca. Rather, beginning in the early 1980s, upscale clothing outlets begin to locate in the area, bringing many changes to Manchester. These are not typical outlet activities, however. The stores are high-end retail outlets such as Ralph Lauren, Donna Karan, Brooks Brothers, J. Crew, Calvin Klein, and even the first Giorgio Armani factory outlet (Coy 1993).

Thus, Manchester differs from the majority of the towns featured in this book. It has not suffered a long-term economic decline and never had a major industrial base, so declines in manufacturing did not prompt an effort to attract retail outlets to boost its economy. Rather, it has been a relatively quiet, elegant summer resort village.

Developing the Concept

In the early 1980s, high-end retail outlets began to converge on Manchester. The advent of New York's Seventh Avenue apparel manufacturers setting up factory outlets has literally spurred a cultural phenomenon of outlet shopping (DeCaro 1997). Shoppers are attracted to areas such as Manchester by the prospect of high-end retail bargains, or by the perception of bargains. Local government and community leaders quickly decided that they must respond with protective commercial zoning and design standards or risk losing the character of their village with the influx of shoppers and new commercial development. The Manchester Planning and Zoning Department has assumed a lead role in protecting the town, while respecting citizens' needs for economic development and preserving natural resources and local character. As the planning director describes, "Our bottom line in all planning is that short-term gains that ignore long-term costs are not tolerated" (Krohn 2001).

The key to retaining the traditional character of Manchester has been to articulate the town's goals and use a strong design review and planning process to ensure that development plans adhere to the town's overall vision (Albers 2000). Strip shopping centers and malls are disallowed under zoning regulations, and development is directed into the downtown. How does the Planning Department direct all the demands that growth places on Manchester? The citizens, business and civic leaders, and local officials all have a voice in what happens to their town. This broad coalition has led to community consensus on many goals, primarily the preservation of what makes Manchester unique, while gaining benefits of controlled economic growth. This mindset toward community is reflected in the Community Vision for Manchester: "We, the residents of Manchester, have a vision of our town. We believe we can shape our destiny if we can agree on goals, and cooperate to achieve them" (Krohn 2001).

When Manchester was faced with the decision to allow rapid growth to continue or to control and direct it to avoid sprawl, they wisely selected the latter. The community leaders also realized that high-end retail offered job opportunities for residents and that sale tax revenue increases would help the town's budget. Thus, the community decided to embrace the new businesses and establish guidelines to direct growth. One extremely important element is the preservation of the classic village pattern (see Photograph 4.1 for an example of adaptive reuse of a historic structure). Through establishment of stringent design standards, Manchester has been able to keep development pedestrian oriented and in harmony with New England architectural tradition. For example, the town adopted a sixteen-page sign ordinance in 1986 to limit visual pollution and other effects of unmitigated commercial signage. One of the new developments was recently cited as a best practices example: A new franchise gas and convenience store was constructed close to the street, with a sidewalk (Vermont Forum on Sprawl 2001). The gas pumping takes place on the side of the property, not the front as with typically designed stations. The architectural style blends in flawlessly.

Thus, Manchester has successfully integrated new retail and other commercial development into a traditional resort village environment. Their concept of resort shopping has successfully created jobs and increased tax revenues. Yet, their success goes far beyond these two economic measures, it reflects a strong and innovative approach to protect and enhance resources through community participatory planning. The implementation and enforcement of strong development guidelines is a major asset. Their foresight in doing so sets them apart from many other communities.

Outcomes

With the increased commercial activity, transportation issues have arisen in Manchester. To keep downtown pedestrian oriented, the community has created a park-and-walk program to create off-street links between properties and parking lots (Vermont Forum on Sprawl 2001:2). When a developer approached the town about installing a traffic light on a main road, the community responded with an in-

Photograph 4.1
Adaptive Reuse of Historic Structures for Up-Scale Shopping, Manchester, Vermont

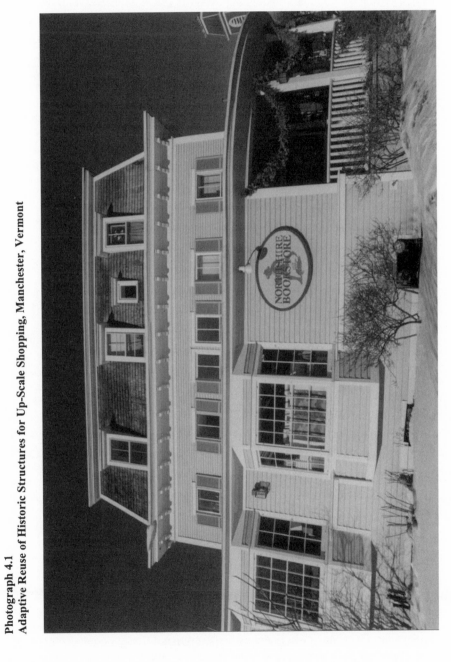

Courtesy of Lee Krohn, Town of Manchester, Vermont.

novative solution: create the state's first roundabout that serves as a gateway to the community, calming traffic as it enters the commercial core. Traffic keeps moving, averting the problems of stopping traffic at a light. Manchester has also conducted "undevelopment"—converting commercial and other spaces into more natural space. A former car dealer lot was cleared and redeveloped into a traditional town green.

The effect of responsible planning is clear in Manchester: the most intensive commercial development occurs downtown rather than in malls on the outskirts of town that encourage a sprawling development pattern (see Photograph 4.2). New development is built next to the sidewalk in traditional New England architectural style. Some historic structures have been renovated to accommodate new businesses as well. Parking is inconspicuous, with the landscaping and placement oriented towards the pedestrian, not the automobile. Sales tax revenues have increased, placing Manchester in the top 5 percent in the state. The outcome is that the village remains attractive, even with much new development, and the three million visitors that frequent the area each year enjoy the combination of this traditional resort village with high-end retail shopping opportunities.

THEMES

This category of towns and cities have utilized retail-based economic development to build community marketing concepts based on themed, or speciality, approaches. Antiquing as a hobby and interest has increased dramatically among the baby boomer generation. As more of this age group retires, traveling to destinations to pursue antiquing is becoming more popular. Several towns have seized on this opportunity and have literally transformed their economies based on retailing antiques. Havana, Florida, and Walnut, Iowa, are two notable examples. Wooster, Ohio, is using another themed approach, that of an old-fashioned downtown experience, incorporating historic structures as well as cultural attractions to boost retail activities. It is also an excellent example of how The Main Street Program has been successfully used to develop a community marketing concept. Vacaville, California is a hybrid of themed and outlet approaches, attempting to maintain its outlet destination status while revitalizing its downtown with specialty retail.

VACAVILLE, CALIFORNIA
POPULATION: 84,000
CONCEPT: OUTLETS AND DOWNTOWN RETAIL

This city located halfway between Sacramento and San Francisco has extensively used retail as a basis for its economic development. It not only utilizes outlet mall development to garner additional tax revenues and growth, it also aggressively promotes downtown revitalization using retail. This unusual and noteworthy combination is a viable case for examination. The city's efforts in downtown

Photograph 4.2
Resort Shopping, Manchester, Vermont

Courtesy of Lee Krohn, Town of Manchester, Vermont.

revitalization are modeled in part after San Antonio, Texas, with the marketing concept of "A Creek Runs Through It," to reflect the development of the waterway in the center of downtown.

In 1841, the Mexican government awarded a large land grant to Manuel Vaca and Felipe Pena. In 1859, most of the land was sold and a one square mile area was used as the town site for Vacaville (Vacaville Chamber of Commerce 2000). The rich soil of the area proved to be ideal for growing fruit and nut orchards as well as grain crops and attracted settlers. Population was 1,500 when the city was incorporated in 1892 and remained at that level until the 1940s. The city remembers its historical roots and celebrates Fiesta Days each year, with the first recorded celebration in 1848.

The fruit industry was the mainstay of the economy, with Vacaville producing half of all California's deciduous fruits into the early twentieth century. After World War I, other areas in California begin to irrigate fruit crops and Vacaville could no longer compete.

Impetus for Change

Agriculture begin to decline as the mainstay of the economy in the 1920s and 1930s and the population of the area did not grow. With World War II came many changes, including the establishment of a large U.S. Air Force base. In the 1950s, the State of California opened a medical and psychiatric center for prisoners. With the advent of both these developments, the population of Vacaville increased to over 9,000 by 1957 (Vacaville Chamber of Commerce 2000:2). Population continued to increase as California grew. By 1970, over 21,000 persons lived in the city; in 1980 over 43,000; and by 1990, 71,000.

Even with the dramatic increase in population, Vacaville virtually had no retail establishments. With the passing of Proposition 13 in 1978 in California, which placed limitation on property taxes, the generation of sales tax became vitally important. Every city's and county's budget shrunk because of the limits placed on property taxes. The attention of local government then shifted to retail and the generation of sales tax to recoup lost property tax revenues. Vacaville's budget was severely impacted by Proposition 13 because of its lack of retail establishments; thus, the city focused its attention on enticing retail-based development.

Developing the Concept

Vacaville already had the seed for retail in the community, a popular roadside stop called The Nut Tree on the freeway. This began as a fruit stand and quickly developed into an attraction that brought two million tourists per year (Palombo 2000). It also created an identity for the area that was recognized throughout the region. In 1986, a company approached The Nut Tree owners with an idea to develop a 200,000-square-foot outlet mall. In 1988 it opened with 56 stores and was instantly successful, and expanded quickly to over 400,000 square feet of retail space (Hamilton 1993).

During the next few years, over two million square feet of retail space was developed along the freeway corridor, securing Vacaville's role as an outlet destination. Eventually, the original Nut Tree tourist attraction closed, and the city purchased the property with the intention of redeveloping it for value-oriented retail. Other retail establishments began to move into the area, particularly "big-box" retail such as Target, Walmart SuperStore, Old Navy, and Mervyn's (Gingerich 2000).

The private land owners and developers played a major role in redirecting Vacaville's future retail. However, the City of Vacaville has been instrumental in developing retail too. They offered a variety of incentives to entice retail-based enterprises and invested $10 million in supporting infrastructure (Palombo 2000). The city did not impose major development or impact fees, as did many other California cities, thus earning a very business friendly reputation. The city has also exhibited progressive thinking in developing a comprehensive Capital Improvement Program for a twenty-year period (City of Vacaville 2000). Many cities do not incorporate capital budgeting into their planning efforts, and few for as long as twenty years. In essence, the Capital Improvement Program indicates that the necessary infrastructure to support growth and development has been identified and financing and implementation plans have been scheduled and adopted. This reassures businesses interested in locating or expanding in a community that their infrastructure needs will be met.

The new retail development along the freeway corridor established Vacaville as a retail and outlet center. The traditional downtown area suffered, and the realization dawned that serious efforts would have to be made if downtown were to be kept economically viable. About 1995, the city began to focus on downtown and directed their Redevelopment Department to begin working on revitalization efforts. In 1996, the Redevelopment Agency funded the Downtown Business Association to market and promote the downtown (McManus 2000). Their activities include preservation of historic structures; beautification, including placement of public art in the area; development of public safety; promotional events; and educational seminars. They have also established a Business Improvement District that allows a higher percentage of sales tax revenues to be kept by the city in the redevelopment district. Their first three years were funded by a city grant of $60,000; beginning in 2000 they receive revenues from business taxes and fund-raising events.

Another major activity aimed at revitalizing downtown is the development of the Creek Walk." Hoping to build on a concept similar to that used for San Antonio, Texas' famed River Walk, the $3 million Creek Walk project will enhance Ulatis Creek with botanical features. It also will serve as a focal point for the history of Vacaville. In essence, it is being developed to increase pedestrian traffic in downtown by serving as a natural and heritage attraction, drawing in customers for downtown businesses (McManus 2000:2).

Outcomes

Vacaville has achieved its original mission of building retail to capture sales tax revenues. In 1986, when serious efforts began to incorporate retail into the overall planning and development of the city, sales tax revenues were $1.5 million (Palombo 2000). In 1999, sales tax revenues were $10 million. At least 5,000 jobs in the retail sector have been added as well (Palombo 2000:2). Most of these results emanate from the outlet and big box retail development along the freeway corridor.

Downtown's redevelopment efforts are in progress; thus, definitive outcomes will not be realized for several years. However, initial results are promising: weekend pedestrian traffic through downtown has increased 25 to 30 percent over the last year (McManus 2000). The city is developing zoning ordinances to encourage more retail speciality shops, such as boutiques, to locate downtown. The Downtown Business Association organized and held twenty Friday night concerts in downtown and seventeen Saturday events—all increasing the volume of pedestrians in the area. Approximately 4,000 persons attended each Friday night concert, and merchants reported higher business activity following these events (McManus 2000:2). The association has been instrumental in working with the city to design and implement a series of business incentive programs for downtown (The Downtown Business Association 2000):

- Design assistance grants: Ranging from $500 to $4,500, these grants help to offset business owners' design costs associated with rehabilitation of downtown buildings.
- Façade loans: This program provides fifteen-year term, 3 percent interest loans up to $20,000 for renovation of building facades, including signage, landscaping, painting, and other improvements.
- Historic district building loans: A loan program for buildings located within the historic boundaries of downtown, it provides up to $135,000 at 3 percent interest for a twenty-five-year term.

Vacaville's interesting approach attempts to construct a marketing concept based on the Creek Walk to revitalize downtown, while continuing to maintain its reputation as an outlet destination. It will be interesting to see if the outlet shoppers also visit the downtown area, or if the downtown will primarily draw from the local population.

HAVANA, FLORIDA
POPULATION: 1,806
CONCEPT: NORTH FLORIDA'S ANTIQUE CAPITAL

Named after Havana, Cuba, this small town is located twelve miles north of the state capital, Tallahassee. Why "Havana"? Because the major crop and economic mainstay for many decades was a premium grade of cigar wrapper tobacco grown in the area. Thus, Havana was born of the cigar industry and incorporated as a town in 1906. A railroad linked Havana to Tallahassee and other points throughout the region, helping it grow as a specialty agricultural center.

Until the early 1970s, the shade tobacco grown in the area supported the development of Havana as a small retail and service center for farmers. Warehouses and other support facilities were constructed early in the twentieth century to support the heavy volume of tobacco production. Cattle raising and produce farms were other activities of the area. In 1934, members of the local booster club, The Havana Luncheon Club, decided to embark on a mission to boost the local economy (Witt 2000). They persuaded the owners of a small canning and preserving company to relocate from Chaires, Florida, to Havana. The Havana Canning Company was established to process locally grown fruits and vegetables, and in 1943, a brick and steel building was constructed (Witt 2000:5). Until the early 1960s, the company processed millions of pounds of locally grown produce and served as a major employer in the area.

In 1928, The Planter's Exchange began manufacturing fertilizer for the tobacco growers and produce farmers in the region. Now listed on the National Register of Historic Places, the building is representative of the historic properties that can be found in Havana. After a devastating fire in 1916 leveled the town, brick buildings were constructed that now provides the town with a charming ambience that differs from the wooden structures found in many older small towns in Florida.

Impetus for Change

Havana flourished as a specialty agricultural center in the earlier years. The Havana Canning Company ceased operations in 1962, and the decline of agriculture as the area's economic base accelerated. By the 1970s, the shade tobacco market had declined and growers no longer found it profitable to continue.

This self-described "two-stoplight town" all but died. The once bustling downtown was nearly vacant; as the town's president of the Havana Historical Society describes: "[Havana] . . . just about rolled up its sidewalks. For two decades the town was quiet" (Witt 2000:1). The warehouses and processing facilities that served the agricultural industries were no longer used. The town seemed destined to meet the fate of numerous U.S. small towns once dependent on agriculture: a place with a history and no future.

Developing the Concept

The process of developing Havana as an antiques center and using this specialty retail as a basis for community development began purely as a private sector venture. A local couple decided to buy an entire block in downtown Havana in 1983. The intent was to rent space to a number of antique dealers, an idea they had seen in their frequent travels throughout the United States. Keith Henderson describes the beginning of Havana's new future: "We had begun to see this type of retailing of antiques happening all around the country and found that the idea of renting space to a number of dealers was a better draw for customers" (Henderson 2000).

Photograph 4.3
Antiquing, Havana, Florida

Courtesy of Jennifer Moreau.

In 1984, the shops opened with just four antique dealers, and development grew rapidly from this modest beginning (see Photograph 4.3).

More stores and buildings were purchased and renovated as antique shops as the idea grew that Havana could capture a large market of shoppers. Buildings are typically subdivided, with space leased to a number of dealers. Given its close proximity to Tallahassee, local merchants realized they could draw in the urban crowd with Havana's small town ambience. Some of the antique dealers pooled money to buy billboard space.

As the concept grew, the local chamber of commerce decided to sponsor special events and festivals to encourage larger number of visitors to Havana. Now, the Pumpkin Festival, the Bead Festival, Halloween events, and Christmas activities draw visitors and shoppers from many areas throughout the year. In 2000, twenty-six businesses joined together to form The Historic Havana Advertising Group to further promote the town's retail opportunities (Beare 2000). With a budget of $60,000, this group prints brochures and advertises the town on billboards, television, radio, and newspapers in North Florida, South Georgia, and South Alabama (Beare 2000:2). The group also secured a grant from Florida Power and Enterprise Florida to build a Website to further promote Havana. The local newspaper, *The Havana Herald*, publishes an advertising paper, *The Havana Merchant*, several times a year to serve visitors to the area.

Another impressive outgrowth of citizens and business owners banding together has been the formation of the MusicFest. Beginning in 1997, this yearly jazz festival has featured major musical artists such as Herbie Mann and Chuck Mangione. Local and regional artists also are included in the festival. Approximately 5,000 to 6,000 people attend the MusicFest each March (Town of Havana 2000).

The town's government later began to support the private sector efforts by providing some landscaping and infrastructure improvements (Henderson 2000). There are also efforts to develop a Main Street Program for Havana, a downtown revitalization program offered through the National Trust for Historic Preservation. A Main Street Program would help to further refine redevelopment and improvement efforts in the downtown area. The City of Havana also received a grant for $500,000 for streetscaping, including the installation of old-fashioned lampposts and other amenities to support redevelopment (Beare 2000). Photograph 4.4 shows how the streetscaping creates a pleasant ambience for shopping.

Outcomes

For a town that seemed destined to become a memory, Havana has reinvented itself as a specialty retail destination. Using antiques as the drawing card, the local merchants built a basis for attracting shoppers from a large region. Banding together to advertise Havana's attractions has served the community well, with a steady increase in sales and tax revenues. The benefits are clear: the town has greater revenues to improve the quality of services for its citizens and can plan for the future. With tax revenues collected increasing 40 percent from 1990 to 2000 (Florida Department of Revenue 2000), Havana now has a more stable financial basis. Table 4.1 illustrates the increase in sales and taxes generated (Florida Department of Revenue 2000:1).

Photograph 4.4
The Ambiance of Antiquing, Havana, Florida

Courtesy of Jennifer Moreau.

The businesses have enjoyed the expanded activities too. The original developer of the antique retailing concept reported that sales were at least ten times greater than in 1984 (Henderson 2000). Havana has successfully reoriented its future, and retail has been a major component of its community revitalization.

Table 4.1
Sales and Tax Revenues for Havana

Year	Gross Sales	Taxes Collected
1990	$39,419,146	$1,505,180
1995	$53,738,073	$1,680,744
2000	$87,132,517	$2,103,569

Source: Florida Department of Revenue 2000.

WALNUT, IOWA
POPULATION: 900
CONCEPT: IOWA'S ANTIQUE CITY

Officially designated by the state's governor as Iowa's Antique City, Walnut is truly a success story of retail-based community concept marketing and revitalization. It has developed into one of the Upper Midwest's most popular tourist attractions. In 1868, the Rock Island Railroad built the Walnut Creek Station. With gently rolling prairie land available for $5 to $10 per acre, settlers rapidly flowed to the area and to the railroad town now called Walnut (Walnut Merchants Association 2001). By 1878, the population was 1,000 and continued to grow to a high of 1,200 in the early twentieth century. The fertile land of the prairie was ideal for farming, and the town was well situated to serve the surrounding area's commercial needs.

Located between Omaha and Des Moines, Walnut became a lively prairie town. Shortly after the turn of the twentieth century, Walnut was described as "a bustling prairie town with several general stores, confectioneries, millenaries, a harness shop, blacksmith, flour mill and an opera house" (Davis 1997:8).

Impetus for Change

Many small towns in the United States established on the basis of agriculture enjoyed economic prosperity until the decline of the industry beginning in the 1960s and accelerating in the 1970s and beyond. Walnut was no exception—thriving in the early years with a large flour mill, bustling downtown district serving a regional hinterland, and even a Model T automobile assembler (Walnut Merchants Association 2001). However, with the departure of the railroad and the shift away from reliance on agriculture Walnut faced an uncertain future, and by the early 1980s, many downtown buildings were boarded up and fell into disrepair. The bustling prairie town of the early 1900s had only one retail business operating in the downtown business district in 1982 (Davis 1997) and the local restaurant was planning to close its doors.

What is unique about Walnut is its ability to thrive and prosper, when similarly situated communities became ghost towns (Davis 1997). Instead of meeting the fate that seemed inevitable, community leaders and citizens of Walnut decided to change the course of their town's future.

Developing the Concept

In 1982, the height of the decline of Walnut, someone suggested that the community could try to develop itself as a tourist attraction. Apparently, the daughter of one of the antique dealers located in Walnut took a trip to Galena, Illinois (Ranney 2001). There, she saw an antique walk that attracted many people to the community. She returned to Walnut and enthusiastically presented the idea to others. At first, some were skeptical and thought Walnut was far too small to embark on such an ambitious plan. Enough of the citizenry were dissatisfied with the continuing economic decline of Walnut and decided to try to help build Walnut as an antiques shoppers' destination.

The first Antique Show and Christmas Walk were organized and held in 1982. Although the crowd was small, around 500 persons, these events signaled the beginning of the re-creation of Walnut's economy into one built on retail and tourism (Walnut Area Development Association 1999). Several more antique dealers moved into the downtown area, and the direction was set. Meetings were held to discuss how Walnut could be transformed into a destination town. In 1983, the local chapter of a national organization, AMVETS, organized the Annual AMVETS Antique Show and Walk on Father's Day weekend. It is now the largest annual event in Walnut, with over 350 antique dealers and 40,000 to 45,000 visitors over the three-day event (Ranney 2001). Photograph 4.5 provides a view of Walnut during one of these events. Several organizations formed—including the Merchants Association, The Community Club, and later, the Walnut Area Development Association—to promote growth and development of the town and the surrounding area.

That same year, local officials conducted an appraisal of Walnut's assets and found several building blocks for supporting the emerging concept. The town enjoyed an advantageous location near the interstate between two major cities. There were several late nineteenth- and early twentieth-century buildings, an auction house in good condition, an attractive entryway to the town, and the original brick and stone streets (Davis 1997). A common vision was identified and published in 1984. The vision statement is specific, and is a great example of how a community can come together to project a common future by articulating its goals and objectives. Visioning can be a powerful process for a community, and in Walnut's case, it served to unite the community in its development efforts. The vision statement is reproduced below:

We have a vision for the future. It involves Walnut, Iowa. In our vision, Walnut thrives and prospers during a period when other communities of Walnut's size in rural America have become, or are becoming, ghost towns. Walnut thrives because it discovered an industry to which it is ideally suited and the whole community is working together to cause that industry to focus on Walnut. That industry is, "Tourism." In our vision, virtually the entire

Photograph 4.5
Antique Fair, Walnut, Iowa

Main Street of Walnut is lined with business enterprises that are attractive to tourists. The primary theme is the antique and collectibles shops that line both sides of the streets. However, motels, country inns, restaurant, dinner theaters, old fashioned soda foundation, country saloons with live entertainment, bed and breakfast or anything else "country," all will fit our vision. In our vision of the future the City Council has changed the name of the Main Street to "Antique Lane," and Pottawattamie County has also adopted the name and extended it north of Walnut beyond the Freeway exit. With help from the Iowa Departments of Tourism and Transportation, the exit signs on I-80 for Walnut now read, "Exit 46—Walnut—Iowa's Antique City." In our vision, each week during the tourist season, thousands of automobiles take that exit and the occupants all enjoy a visit to a truly delightful country town. The industry has created jobs that in turn increased business for the non tourism oriented businesses like the insurance agencies, the telephone company, the grocery store and the real estate firms. (Walnut Area Development Association 1999:7)

Outcomes

The vision statement of 1984 describes the Walnut of 2001 almost perfectly. The citizens, government officials, and business owners began in earnest to make the vision a reality, and in conjunction with several organizations started building the concept. These organizations include The Community Club, The Walnut Area Development Association, The Optimist Club, The AMVETS Post No. 45, and The Merchants Association. Each has made a major contribution and all have worked together to achieve impressive outcomes for a town the size of Walnut. For example, The Optimist Club conducted a fund-raising effort and gathered $70,000 for a conversion and remodeling of the old fire station into the Walnut Visitors Center. The local government contributes about $6,000 per year for its operation. The local government also funds a Christmas light display each year, and in 1991, installed antique light fixtures in downtown to enhance the antique town ambience (Ransom 2000). Other improvements include adding a painted mural to the downtown streetscape (see Photograph 4.6). The Walnut Area Development Association worked to have bus tours stop in Walnut, bringing numerous visitors on a regular basis to the community.

The Main Street, now renamed Antique City Drive, and the surrounding area are now home to numerous antique dealers—one source counted as many as 250 dealers. The antiques businesses have been the key to Walnut's revived economy. Additionally, support services have been developed to serve the tourists. These include four gas stations; two motels; three bed and breakfast inns; three quick-serve restaurants, including a McDonald's; five full-service restaurants; and fifteen general services businesses (Walnut Area Development Association 2001).

Advertising for Walnut is now handled by The Merchants Association. With a budget of $20,000 annually, they promote Walnut throughout the region (Ranney 2001). They were also instrumental in changing Main Street's name and having it placed on the interstate exit sign. This helped tremendously to pull traffic from the interstate (Ransom 2000). AMVETS spends about $30,000 annually on advertising and support for conducting the annual Antique Walk, which is Walnut's single largest event each year.

On one end of Antique City Drive is the newly renovated Walnut Creek Historical Museum, operated by the Walnut Historical Society. On the other end is the Walnut Country Opera House. The producer of the Front Street Theater in Dodge City, Kansas, acquired the Opera House in 1999 and refurbished it (Walnut Area Development Association 2001). Productions are held biweekly, usually to a full house. A national hotel chain approached the town in 1998 to develop a convention center and golf course. The local government used tax increment financing funds to provide the supporting infrastructure.

It is estimated that as many as 250,000 tourists and shoppers visit Walnut each year. The impact on this town of 900 persons is dramatic. Tax revenues have increased substantially and property values have increased. Additional revenues help to support quality of life improvements, such as an expansion to the elementary school. Some of the highest per capita sales taxes in the state emanate from Walnut (Ranney 2001). Several new residents have moved to Walnut, and the town is enjoying a new vibrancy. Buildings that were vacant in the 1980s are now occupied with thriving enterprises, and the community's future is more assured.

Photograph 4.6
Mural Painting by Tom Walker, Walnut, Iowa

WOOSTER, OHIO
POPULATION: 25,000
CONCEPT: OLD-FASHIONED DOWNTOWN EXPERIENCE

Wooster serves as the gateway to the largest Amish community in the United States. Because of its location, large crowds of tourists are enticed to journey to this rural area of North Central Ohio. Wooster serves as the service center for Wayne County, with slightly over 100,000 in population. Of these, approximately 25,000 are Amish, representing eighty-three church congregations (Wooster Area Chamber of Commerce 2000).

Three surveyors explored the interior of Ohio, and in 1808 staked claims to land that today is Wooster. The town was named for General David Wooster, a Revolutionary War officer. Settlers began to locate in the Wooster area because of its rich soil, and in 1817 the town was incorporated. When the railroads laid track through Wayne County beginning in the 1850s, Wooster began to develop industry. By the late 1800s, Wooster was home to grist mills, tanneries, a steam-engine plant, a farm equipment manufacturer, and the Wooster Brush Company (Spectrum Publications 2000). In 1870, the University of Wooster, now known as the College of Wooster, opened its doors.

Impetus for Change

Like many mid-sized towns across the United States, Wooster began to lose its traditional downtown retail and other commercial activities. The shopping malls of Canton and Akron served as powerful draws for local citizens, and when a strip mall was developed at Wooster's northern end, downtown retail's decline was hastened. By the mid-1980s, vacancy rates downtown were over 40 percent (Hull 2000).

In 1985, the community leaders in Wooster decided to organize their revitalization efforts and created Main Street Wooster, Inc., a nonprofit entity. Part of the nationwide Main Street Program operated by the National Trust for Historic Preservation, this new organization focused on revitalizing the downtown core. All sectors of the community have been involved, with representatives from local government, professional and manufacturing entities, and downtown business and property owners.

Developing the Concept

Wooster had a resource that proved to be extremely valuable in its efforts to halt the decline: Rubbermaid Incorporated. The corporate headquarters of Rubbermaid are located in Wooster. The company was founded in 1934 to produce rubber houseware products. By 1941, sales were $685,000 annually (Hull 1994); by 2000 this international corporation employed approximately 2,000 and had sales in the billions. In 1989, one of the last anchors of the commercial district went out of business—a 106-year-old family-operated department store. The owners donated the 33,000-square-foot building to the city, and a group of twenty local investors financed its renovation (Johnson and Broughton 1996). Rubbermaid was looking for a site for a new laboratory marketing store, Everything Rubbermaid, in which retail customers could shop for more than 3,000 Rubbermaid products and provide valuable feedback to the manufacturer (Johnson and Broughton 1996:4). The renovated department store seemed ideal, and "the result is an unparalleled downtown retail complex that lures more than 200 tour buses each year and nearly half a million shoppers from as far away as Japan and Australia" (Johnson and Broughton 1996:4). Everything Rubbermaid serves as a centerpiece for other commercial investment and growth.

Wooster's revitalization efforts have truly been a community-wide partnership, with several programs that have helped the downtown become a vital center once again. These programs include (Hull 1994):

- establishment of a loan pool and participation loan agreements with low interest rates;
- architectural and design assistance available on a fifty-fifty cost basis for restoration or
- rehabilitation of downtown buildings; and
- establishment of a realtor network and recruitment program to attract new businesses into downtown.

The Main Street Wooster, Inc., organization has been instrumental in orchestrating downtown's economic resurgence. Its vision statement has catalyzed the community to support development of Wooster's concept as an old-fashioned downtown experience: "Downtown Wooster is the cornerstone of the community dedicated to the development of public/private partnerships, maintenance of small town tradition, development of specialized retail, professional, and governmental business/offices, and celebration through events" (Main Street Wooster, Inc. 1995). This statement articulates the four themes for Wooster's development plans: public/private partnerships, small town tradition, specialized retail and other businesses, and celebration.

Outcomes

Wooster has achieved a high level of success in realizing its vision for downtown. As of 2000, over $50 million has been reinvested in downtown via public and private funds. From vacancy rates of over 40 percent in the late 1980s, to a vacancy rate of less than 5 percent in 2000, Wooster considers the efforts very rewarding. Others do too, as the National Trust for Historic Preservation selected Wooster for one of the 1996 Great American Main Street Awards.

The State of Ohio, impressed by the activities of Main Street Wooster, Inc., granted $650,000 for downtown streetscaping and façade improvements (Hull

1994). The City of Wooster also invested in improving infrastructure. With a total project cost of $2.8 million, Wooster's business and property owners agreed to pay $1 million of the cost through special assessment. The city also helps manage loan funds.

The partnership with Rubbermaid continues to confer benefits for Wooster. The company was instrumental in recruiting Corning-Revere to open a factory store in downtown Wooster. The combination has spurred additional specialty retail and supporting activities, such as restaurants opening in the downtown. To spur retail-based development even more, a volunteer team canvassed businesses within a seventy-five-mile radius of Wooster to consider opening a branch business in Wooster. This innovative recruitment effort helped increase recognition of Wooster as a vital retail destination. Retail recruitment is a vital component of the revitalization effort, and much of it focuses on retail that would be compatible with the Everything Rubbermaid store (Hull 1994).

Over 100 new businesses have opened in Wooster as a result of the revitalization efforts. Tax revenues have increased, and the vacancy in downtown is now minimal. A local 3 percent hotel occupancy tax helps to fund improvements and also provides some support for The Main Street Wooster, Inc., programs. The ability to develop and sustain the concept of Wooster as an old-fashioned downtown experience has been successful, and with strong public-private partnerships will likely persevere into the future.

SUMMARY

Retail as a community economic development strategy? Absolutely. This chapter illustrates the approaches to integrating retail into community economic development thus serving as the basis for developing community concept marketing approaches. Even though retail has not been traditionally considered a major economic development component of a community's development plans, many communities have begun to seriously consider retail in this regard, given the successes of communities that have already embraced retail. For communities that are not able to sustain or attract manufacturing or other types of employment activities, retail can serve as a viable alternative to stabilizing and enhancing local economies. For communities that already have other economic activities, retail can further encourage community development.

The six communities profiled present various approaches to using retail to build a concept community marketing approach. While one community aggressively pursued recruitment and expansion of retail outlet establishments, another in which the resort shopping concept was purely accidental decided to make the most of it. Virtually all the communities strive to enhance retail in their downtown areas, with retail considered the most viable approach to ensuring their downtown's future. Several ideas and innovations identified in these communities' concept marketing approaches hold relevance for other towns and cities. When a community begins to explore the idea of using retail to build a concept, there are several aspects to consider:

1. Is the community's location conducive to attracting large numbers of shoppers?
   - How far away are interstates or other major transportation arteries?
   - If the location is isolated, are there mitigating factors that could make retail feasible, such as a natural or cultural attraction or a nearby tourist attraction?
2. Can the community's infrastructure support increased vehicular traffic?
   - Is public parking available?
   - What problems will increased traffic cause for the community?
3. Is there supporting infrastructure in place to serve large numbers of visitors?
   - Are there public facilities available?
   - Are there adequate hotel/motel/restaurant services, or room for these activities to be developed?

After these questions are addressed, a community must consider the available resources for developing the concept. Will there be interest from all three sectors, the private, public, and nonprofit? How is the private sector going to respond? Can the interest from retail enterprises be assessed to gauge their interest in locating in the community? Will the community support a concept that generally implies a large number of visitors to the community each year? Are there special environmental considerations or resources that will need protection from increased activity? Is there something unusual or special about the community that can serve as the basis for building the concept? In Wooster, Ohio, the existing old-fashioned downtown proved to be the greatest resource and served as the building block for the marketing concept. Havana, Florida, found that they could utilize their history as a small agricultural town to build their image as North Florida's antiquing capital.

Perhaps most important is the willingness of the local government to take a stand and implement, with community consensus, a solid and protective regulatory framework. A community plan, with zoning and other ordinances that support achievement of community goals can be vital to protecting important assets while allowing responsible growth. The ability of a community to clearly articulate what they want to achieve in their future is powerful. Community visioning, as seen in the case of Walnut, Iowa, can be astounding. The desire to protect and enhance existing resources and ambience through land use and other regulatory measures while gaining the benefits of increased retail activity is clearly illustrated in the case of Manchester, Vermont.

Retail can serve as the basis for a concept marketing approach. A key point in using retail to build the concept is to utilize a feature, asset, or technique that is unique. Antiquing and theming are two methods of accomplishing this. Retail utilized in this manner not only serves as a supplement to other activities, but as the attraction itself.

NOTE

1. This section has been excerpted with permission from the article by Rhonda Phillips, "What Are the Positive Benefits of Retail-Based Economic Growth for Communities?" *Journal of Shopping Center Research* 7, no. 1 (spring/summer 2000): 7–28.

5

Building on Tradition

Traditions, as reflected in ethnic activities or architecture, can provide a powerful foundation on which to build community concept marketing approaches. The ability to parlay latent assets of ethnicity or historic properties into community economic development outcomes has been demonstrated by a host of communities.

HISTORIC PRESERVATION AS COMMUNITY ECONOMIC DEVELOPMENT

Historic preservation as economic development? Quoting Greg Paxton, executive director of the Georgia Trust for Historic Preservation, in the introduction to *The Economics of Historic Preservation* (Rypkema 1994:1): "The economic benefits of historic preservation are enormous. The knowledge of the economic benefits of preservation are minuscule." The mere presence of historic structures in a community alone is not enough to build a concept marketing approach for community revitalization. Involvement and commitment to preserving and restoring the historic buildings, as well as providing supporting and complementary assets in the community, is required. Enhancing "latent" properties as part of an overall marketing and redevelopment approach is a definitive requirement. It goes much further: There must be incentive for private property owners of historic structures to renovate or otherwise upgrade their properties to help provide the background for a community concept marketing approach built on historic preservation. This incentive may be the ability to recoup costs by participating in a revitalized or expanded economy by operating a business, or selling the property at a profit. As Rypkema described, there are many more historic buildings that merit being saved than can possibly be museums. There is simply not enough public funds to preserve all the worthy historic buildings, and "most historic buildings are not owned by historic preservationists" (Rypkema 1994:1).

Communities using historic preservation to build a concept marketing approach do not necessarily have to possess Victorian era or earlier architectural properties. Later styles of architecture and design can form a basis for historic preservation as well. For example, Wildwood, New Jersey, is developing a concept marketing campaign as the Doo Wop Capital of the World (Zuckerman 2000). The basis for this concept is a collection of 1950s and 1960s commercial architecture located in the community. Communities must think creatively about methods to preserve and enhance the built environment of historic structures. These potential uses of structures sometimes are not recognized at first glance, and it requires innovative thought about their potential uses and integration into a community concept marketing approach.

LOOKING TO THE PAST: HERITAGE AND CULTURAL LINKS FOR COMMUNITY ECONOMIC DEVELOPMENT

Heritage or cultural tourism is rapidly gaining interest as a viable community development strategy. Numerous communities have incorporated some element of heritage or cultural tourism into their marketing efforts. Using cultural elements, such as ethnicity, forms the basis of folk festivals, estimated at over three thousand per year in the United States (Gillespie 1987). Described as an "archipelago of cultural displays" these events display a map of ethnic heritage across the United States (Hoelscher 1998:13). Ethnicity, as reflected in the resurgence of interest in vernacular traditions, is now fashionable (Conzen 1990; Harvey 1989; Hoelscher 1998). As Conzen describes (1990: 245), there is an "ethnic reawakening" as communities attempt to reinvigorate their ethnic associations. After years of neglecting ethnicity and heritage in attempts to modernize and mainstream towns and cities, many communities are now using their heritage as a basis for community economic development.

Thousands of communities have one or more annual events that serve to draw large numbers of tourists, such as rural Jonesborough, Tennessee's annual storytelling festival that brings in 8000 visitors from all 50 states and over $5 million in economic impact (Hoke 1996). Most states have at least one living history museum depicting past ways of life, such as The Georgia Agriama in Tifton. Considered one of the most successful heritage museums of its type in the United States, it draws over 60,000 visitors annually to its host rural community (Phillips 1998).

The heritage or cultural links can be broad-based or narrow, depending on the perceived draw of interest from others in the link. For example, The Rural Life Center, located at Louisiana State University in Baton Rouge, provides a variety of cultural artifacts and heritage programs, built on the idea that ten flags have flown over Louisiana. The displays and programs range from interpretive exhibits on voodoo practices to preindustrial farming demonstrations. Other communities focus on one aspect of heritage or culture and market it for maximum return. This is often evident with annual festivals and special events such as those promoting a community as " the _____ capital of the world," inserting the relevant agricultural or food product.

Some of these communities have excelled in developing their heritage or cultural links as a foundation for building community economic development. Viable concept marketing on the basis of historic preservation or ethnicity is continually emerging.

HISTORIC PRESERVATION

Parlaying historic properties into a successful concept marketing approach requires tremendous cooperation, energy, and commitment. Three communities exemplify this dedication to building community revitalization based on historic preservation: Cape May, New Jersey; Natchitoches, Louisiana; and Eureka Springs, Arkansas. While each community's story is different, they share the common characteristic of collaboration between the public and private sectors.

CAPE MAY, NEW JERSEY
POPULATION: 5,000
CONCEPT: VICTORIAN SEASHORE RESORT

Founded in 1630 as a New Netherlands colony, Cape May is the oldest seashore resort in the United States. Substantiating this claim is a rich history. The colony first began as a whaling and fishing center. After the War of 1812, steamboats ferried passengers into the area and the town began to flourish as a resort. Cape May stretches twenty miles into the Atlantic from the southernmost tip of New Jersey. The picturesque setting attracted numerous summertime visitors seeking escape from the oppressive heat of the region's urban areas. In 1830, a writer described the resort:

Cape May Island is a noted and much frequented watering place, the season at which commences about the first of July and continues until the middle of August or the first of September. There are six boarding houses, three of which are very large; the sea bathing is convenient and excellent, the beach affords pleasant drives and there is excellent fishing in adjacent waters. (U.S. Department of Interior 1970:9)

The development of hotels and other service establishments flourished as national and international recognition of Cape May as a seashore resort was gained during the remainder of the nineteenth century. Famous visitors that enhanced its status included Henry Clay, Abraham Lincoln and four other U.S. presidents, John Philip Sousa, and P. T. Barnum. As many as 3,000 visitors per day arrived by steamboat from the 1850s to the 1880s (Patterson 2000). By 1853, it was home to the world's largest hotel, the Mount Vernon; tragically, this hotel along with other famous summer palaces was lost in the disastrous fire of 1967 (Bailey 2000).

Despite damaging fires and storms, nearly 600 nineteenth- and early twentieth-century structures have survived. These historic structures create the unique character of Cape May. The architecture is of the mixed vernacular that produced the picturesque and romantic style of the Victorian era, that incorporated Gothic, Mansard, Italianate, Queen Anne, Eastlake, and Greek Revival traditions. Cape May offers an impressive array of all the popular styles of the nineteenth century. Additionally, many frame buildings constructed in the early twentieth century contributed to the character of the town. Cape May thus claims to be home to the largest collection of nineteenth- and early twentieth-century frame buildings in the United States (Bailey 2000).

Impetus for Change

When Atlantic City, New Jersey, became the seaside resort of choice in the early part of the twentieth century, Cape May fell into an economic decline that lasted nearly fifty years. Many historic structures fell into disrepair and were threatened by other types of development, such as commercial and industrial uses that were incompatible with the character and architecture of the area. The decline continued until the 1960s, when the unparalleled collection of Victorian seaside architecture began to attract historic preservationists and artists. The preservationists and artists were in conflict with the city government officials, envisioned new construction as the future for Cape May. The signal impetus for dramatic change in Cape May came in the summer of 1970, when the historic Hotel Lafayette was torn down to build a new motel (Zuckerman 1998: 219).

The threat of destruction of this and other major historic structures in the town prompted concerned citizens to form a nonprofit organization, the Mid-Atlantic Center for the Arts, with the broad mission of historic preservation and arts-based activities. City hall turned down federal grants secured by this group to purchase historic properties; thus, the group engaged in a "political revolution" to elect a mayor who supported a quality of life and historic preservation platform (Zuckerman 2000).

Developing the Concept

With the new political administration and intense efforts by the Mid-Atlantic Center for the Arts, Cape May turned its future around. The major achievement of this administration was the declaration of Cape May as a National Historic Landmark in 1976. One of only a few in the nation—as of 1999 there were only five in the United States—this designation requires that Cape May retain all structures in their original form and design (Bailey 2000). This ensures that town buildings will remain within the architectural guidelines of the Victorian period. With landmark status came a commitment from city government to a future based on historic preservation. The Historic Preservation Committee, comprised of volunteers, provides regulatory oversight for the city.

Once the public sector's agenda changed to one of support for historic preservation, redevelopment efforts have been undertaken jointly by the nonprofit sector, the city government, and the private sector. The uniqueness of Cape May's rebirth as a Victorian theme seaside resort is exemplified in this joint partnership. Each plays a vital role: the public sector provides the regulatory controls, such as policies, zoning, design ordinances, and other measures as well as the supporting infrastructure; the private sector invests millions of dollars to restore hundreds of historic structures; and the nonprofit sector's ability to build collaborative efforts through the Mid-Atlantic Center for the Arts. It is crucial to note that the development approach Cape May has taken is one of community bootstrapping, in which concerned citizens in all three sectors are the driving force for effecting positive community change (Zuckerman 1998:219). There were no philanthropists to rescue Cape May, as John D. Rockefeller, Jr. did at Colonial Williamsburg; nor has there been major government or state funding, such as the National Park Service's efforts at Philadelphia's Independence National Park (Zuckerman 1998:219). Until 2000, they had never received monies from the New Jersey Historical Commission (Zuckerman 2000).

The Mid-Atlantic Center for the Arts has played a pivotal role in Cape May's re-emergence as a Victorian seaside resort. Their first major effort was to rescue from demolition the vandalized and overgrown Emlen Physick Estate, an 1879 mansion on eight acres (see Photograph 5.1). With financial assistance in the form of a U.S. Department of Housing and Urban Development grant, the group purchased the estate, and after a complete restoration, began operating it as a Victorian house museum (Groff and Weiland 2000).

The Mid-Atlantic Center for the Arts has always held a grander vision of community-wide preservation, restoration, and development for Cape May. Their activities reflect this commitment to encouraging large-scale community improvement. Activities and programs range from organizing historic house tours, trolley tours, and guided walking tours to special events. These latter activities help extend the traditional ten weeks of summer tourism. Seasonal events such as Victorian Weekend during the Columbus Day Holiday, haunted house tours at Halloween, and the Christmas Candlelight House Tour have helped Cape May become a year-round destination (Zuckerman 1998:222).

In addition to these activities, the Mid-Atlantic Center for the Arts performs critical marketing functions for Cape May and serves as its principal marketer. "This Week in Cape May," an informative booklet funded by advertisements, is a free guide for tourists and residents alike (Bailey 2000). The Center also performs other marketing outreach activities, including ticket sales for area theater companies and promotion of the Cape May-Lewes Ferry and shuttle bus from Delaware to various local attractions.

The key to many of these activities that support Cape May's concept as a Victorian seaside resort has been the strong collaborative efforts within the community.

Photograph 5.1
Emlen Physick House, Cape May's Victorian Museum, Cape May, New Jersey

Courtesy of Mid-Atlantic Center for the Arts, Chamber of Commerce of Greater Cape May, New Jersey.

Bolstered by support from both citizens and businesses, the Cape May Music Festival is now a flagship cultural offering (Zuckerman 1998). Partnering with the local association of innkeepers has led to Sherlock Holmes Mystery Weekends in October and March, and a workshop on how to acquire, restore, and operate a bed and breakfast inn that attracts participants from throughout the United States. The restaurateurs in the area joined forces with the Mid-Atlantic Center for the Arts to sponsor the annual Cape May Food and Wine Festival in the early fall. Partnerships with the local government include assistance with operating information booths and co-sponsorship of craft shows and programs at the convention hall.

Outcomes

Cape May's concept marketing approach as a seaside resort has been highly successful, as measured by a variety of factors. Overall, the community has experienced economic and cultural revitalization since 1970, when interest in historic preservation and restoration of the community's collection of Victorian-era architecture first gained momentum. Reversing a population decline, the revitalization efforts have prompted an increase of 30 percent in the summer resident population, from 23,800 to just over 31,000 (Cape May County Planning Board 2000). Although the year-round resident population is still relatively low, it has increased from 4,668 in 1990 to 5,000 in 2000. Cape May's influence extends beyond the city boundaries though—the entire area, Cape May County, has experienced a 35 percent increase in population from 1980 to 2000, from 82,000 to over 111,000 (Cape May County Planning Board 2000). It is expected to continue to grow, with a 25 percent increase over the next twenty years. Not all growth has been prompted by Cape May's success, but it has certainly influenced revitalization efforts in adjacent areas.

The most visible economic impact is tourism. Visitation has increased dramatically since restoration and revitalization efforts began, from less than 50,000 tourists in 1980 to over 350,000 in 1999 (Zuckerman 1998). This sevenfold increase in tourist volume is astounding—few cities of Cape May's size are able to obtain this level of tourism. The impact of increased tourism has led to development of more businesses. According to Cape May County officials, the number of bed and breakfast inns has grown from 2 to over 100 as of 1999 (see Photograph 5.2). Additionally, there are an estimated fifty to seventy-five guest houses operating in Cape May (Groff and Weiland 2000). The commercial sector has grown too, with over 600 businesses operating in Cape May, including a variety of restaurants and other establishments (Groff and Weiland 2000:2). Correspondingly, the number and variety of jobs available to year-round and seasonal residents have increased.

The impact of the nonprofit sector, primarily represented by the Mid-Atlantic Center for the Arts, is felt too. The organization first formed in 1970 by a group of concerned citizens focused on historic preservation. During the years that followed, the Center has grown from a volunteer effort to become one of Cape May's

Photograph 5.2
The Mainstay Inn Bed and Breakfast, Cape May, New Jersey

largest employers, with 30 full-time professional staff and 110 part-time employees (Zuckerman 1998:223).

Eighty percent of the funding for the concept marketing and development of Cape May is provided through revenues from admission tickets to the many sites and events. Additionally, the Center has partnered with the City of Cape May to draw in funds from state organizations, such as the New Jersey Historic Trust ($1 million for restoration of the Cape May Lighthouse), and from federal agencies, such as the U.S. Department of Transportation ($700,000 for transportation improvements to support the Cape May Lighthouse). The private sector has also invested heavily in properties throughout the area. One of the outcomes has been a major increase in property values—homes that sold for $30,000 or less in 1980 are now selling for $600,000 to over $1,000,000 (Groff and Weiland 2000). Accordingly, the city's revenues and tax base have increased, helping to stabilize and expand the public sector's budgets.

Growth and development is not without cost, and issues remain to be resolved as a result of the dramatic increase in visitors to Cape May. One of the most pressing issues is how to address transportation needs, such as parking facilities and alternative modes for improving traffic flows and volumes. Cape May will have to rely on its precedent of public-private collaboration to devise creative solutions to these and other issues resulting from growth and development.

Cape May demonstrates how historic preservation can revitalize a community. Starting with concerted efforts to preserve and restore the built environment, the process grew to encompass activities and programs resulting in increased economic vitality. Overall, the Victorian Seaside Resort concept marketing approach has been highly successful for Cape May.

NATCHITOCHES, LOUISIANA
POPULATION: 17,000
CONCEPT: HISTORIC NATCHITOCHES

Natchitoches (Nak-a-tosh), founded in 1714 by the French, is actually the oldest permanent settlement in the Louisiana Purchase territory. Older even than New Orleans, its rural location in north-central Louisiana has protected its buildings and homes from urban infringement through the centuries. The closest urban areas, Shreveport to the north and Alexandria to the south, are sixty and seventy miles away. The distance has served as an advantage, providing additional protection for Natchitoches' historic built environment from urban infringement (Harper 2000).

La Rivierre du Cannes, as the Cane River area was called by the French, is a thirty-five mile long and six-mile wide river valley. Originally home to one of the most sophisticated societies in the French colonies, the vestiges of this vibrant French culture include Creole-style architecture in the historic buildings in the valley (Natchitoches Parish Tourist Commission 2000b). Natchitoches sits at the Cane River's headwaters, and the large Cane River Lake meanders through downtown and south to Cloutierville.

The entire region, noted for its plantations and Creole culture, is referred to as Cane River Country. Derived from the Spanish term *criollo*, Creole refers to a heritage of multiculturalism and multiethnicity, primarily French and African as well as Spanish, American Indian, and Western European (Cane River National Heritage Commission 2000b). The influence of Creole in this area is rich: "Nowhere is Louisiana's Afro-Creole flavor more sharply accented than in the Cane River Country lying between Derry and Natchitoches" (Chase 1995:S6).

This confluence of cultures provided a matrix for exciting occurrences. One of the most notable is the rise of Marie Therese Coincoin from slave to matriarch of a Creole dynasty and one of the largest landowners in the area. Born to slavery in 1742, she was freed by owner Thomas Metoyer in 1786 and given land (Chase 1995:6). She started an Afro-Creole family of fourteen children who built several large estates, including the restored Melrose plantation, spanning nearly 2,000 acres (Chase 1995:6). This unusual legacy of a former slave who achieved the status of one of the state's largest landowners provides a rich historical point of interest for building cultural tourism in the area.

Impetus for Change

Throughout Louisiana, oil and gas industry extraction and refining activities have been a major factor in the economy. In the past, Natchitoches relied heavily on this industry. Beginning in the 1970s, the industry experienced decline and Natchitoches began to suffer as employment opportunities decreased. The ensuing recession impacted the entire Cane River Country, and its communities began seeking alternative forms of employment.

Natchitoches had a history of tourism, but was not a major tourist destination in the 1970s. This was primarily due to its isolated location away from major highways and interstates and the lack of recognition of the area's unique offerings. Although it boasted the nation's oldest Christmas lights festival, it was not until the late 1980s that the festival received major recognition. The event spurring its recognition, as well as catapulting Natchitoches into the category of a tourist destination, was the filming of *Steel Magnolias*. Bobby Harling, Jr., a native of Natchitoches, and author of *Steel Magnolias* insisted that it be filmed on location in Natchitoches (Harper 2000). The influx of the cast, crew, and tourists impacted Natchitoches in irreversible ways: the town had to serve the visitors by providing accommodations and services, including installing turn signals where none had previously existed (Harper 2000).

At the same time, the State of Louisiana's Department of Transportation built an interstate highway with a bypass four miles from Natchitoches. This transportation link provided the area with desperately needed access, opening up Natchitoches to a flow of vehicular traffic from the greater region, as well as interstate traffic. Coupled with the dramatic impact of the filming of *Steel Magnolias*, the added infrastructure propelled the community into a new level of tourist-related activity. Natchitoches now had the necessary access, via the bypass, and the attention-grabbing event of a major movie filming to start seriously contending for tourists.

Developing the Concept

Developing the concept of Historic Natchitoches did not require deep soul-searching on the part of the community or major attempts to create an identity for the community. Rather, its development was implicit, that is, the resources, although underutilized at the time of the concept marketing initiation, were already in place. It was more a matter of bringing together all the players so that significant accomplishments could be made.

As with many communities faced with major economic development tasks, the citizens of Natchitoches realized collaboration was essential for success. Utilizing resources from all three sectors, the community embarked on a concept marketing and community development approach of Historic Natchitoches. The role of the private sector is usually crucial to the success of any community economic development effort. The private sector of Natchitoches responded to the challenge by investing in property rehabilitation, restoration, and construction. In addition to providing capital for these activities, the business sector has participated with the public and nonprofit sectors in the creation and viable continuation of a National Historic Landmark District that encompasses the entire downtown business district. The thirty-three block Historic Landmark District provides a picturesque setting along the Cane River Lake and incorporates numerous historic churches, commercial buildings, and homes in a mixture of Queen Anne, Victorian, and Creole architectural styles (Cane River National Heritage Area 2000b).

The private sector has participated in other redevelopment activities with the nonprofit sector. The Natchitoches Area Chamber of Commerce has assisted with a variety of activities to promote and market Natchitoches, including the annual Festival of Lights, the oldest continuous Christmas lights festival in the United States (Natchitoches Area Chamber of Commerce 2000). Over 150,000 visitors attend this festival each year, which gained national attention when mentioned in the film *Steel Magnolias* (Harper 2000).

The Association for the Preservation of Historic Natchitoches, an organization formed in the early 1950s, is a nonprofit entity that participates in helping the community actualize its concept marketing approach. Focused on acquiring historic properties for preservation, the association has impacted the region in many positive ways by preserving cultural and architectural resources. One of the Association's properties is Melrose Plantation, acquired in 1971 and declared a National Historic Landmark in 1974 (Association for the Preservation of Historic Natchitoches 2000). Melrose was the home of Marie Therese Coincoin, the freed slave who became one of the region's largest landowners. While the association focuses its activities on preservation, it serves as a valuable partner for Natchitoches's community concept marketing strategy by providing venues for tourists.

Public sector activity has been equally important in promoting the development of the concept for the community. The City of Natchitoches has actively pursued preservation and development of the downtown National Historic Landmark District as well as other properties and supporting programs. A state representative for the area was instrumental in securing funding for Natchitoches's preservation and development efforts. Due to these efforts, a rebate on the state sales tax has been accruing since 1991, amounting to over $750,000, with annual rebates at $200,000 (Harper 2000). The city formed the Historic District Development Commission to use the funds for programs such as façade grants, retail development grants, and overall beautification and infrastructure improvement of the downtown district (Harper 2000:2).

The efforts at the community level did not go unnoticed, and its historic preservation success prompted the National Park Service to purchase properties located along the Cane River. Oakland and Magnolia Plantations, with over forty-seven historic buildings, family and plantation records, tools, furniture, equipment, and other items were purchased in the early 1990s (Cane River National Heritage Commission 2000a). These two plantations constitute the Cane River Creole National Historical Park, established by the United States Congress in 1994. A part of the National Park System, "the sites demonstrate the history of colonization, frontier influences, French Creole architecture, cotton agriculture, slavery and tenancy labor systems, changing technologies, and evolving social practices over two hundred years" (Cane River National Heritage Commission 2000a:1).

The National Park Service then formed the Cane River National Heritage Commission, an entity regulated by the City of Natchitoches and funded by the federal government, for managing the park and related activities. Further, the entire area surrounding the park has been declared a heritage area by Congress. The Cane River National Heritage Area encompasses 45,000 acres in a thirty-five-mile swath on both sides of the Cane River Lake and features the following attractions in addition to the Cane River Creole National Historic Park: three State Commemorative Areas, including an original 1714 French fort; five National Historic Landmark sites, including the thirty-three-block downtown City of Natchitoches' National Historic Landmark District; and numerous privately owned historic homes and buildings (Cane River National Heritage Commission 2000b).

The combined historic preservation efforts of all three sectors of the community, and the attraction of state and federal interest and funding has led to the development of Natchitoches and the Cane River area as a significant tourist destination. An outgrowth of the preservation and restoration of historic properties has been the conception and implementation of a variety of fairs, special events, and festivals. For example, the Melrose Plantation Arts and Crafts Festival is held on the grounds of the Cane River Creole National Historic Park and attracts over 12,000 visitors. Building on its past as an artists' and writers' retreat and former home to Louisiana's most celebrated primitive artist (Association for the Preservation of Historic Natchitoches 2000), the festival features works of more than 150 artists.

Over sixteen fairs, festivals, and special events are now held each year in Natchitoches Parish (Natchitoches Convention and Visitors Bureau 2000). According to marketing information, thirty-four attractions in the area serve as tourist venues (Natchitoches Convention and Visitors Bureau 2000:2)—many of these sites host fairs, festivals, and special events, incorporating cultural and historic links.

Since 1988, Natchitoches has accelerated its concept marketing and development approach. The number of historic properties, sites, venues, and festivals and other special events is impressive for a community of its size. Its accomplishments are a tribute to the collaborative partnerships in the community.

Outcomes

The economy and the community of Natchitoches have been impacted in a variety of ways by the concept marketing approach of historic preservation and the resulting economic development activities. Activities that service tourists have grown dramatically. For example, in 1984, before tourism had become a major influence, Natchitoches was home to one hotel with 130 rooms. In 2000, there were nine hotels with over 600 rooms, plus 30 bed and breakfast inns with 95 rooms (Harper 2000). Many of the latter are in restored historic properties, further contributing to the preservation and restoration of valuable historic resources. While an official count has not been made, it is estimated that over 800,000 tourists visit Natchitoches and its attractions, festivals, and fairs each year (Natchitoches Convention and Visitors Bureau 2000).

In the 1980s, sales tax revenues for the city were about $500,000 per year. By 2000, sales tax revenues have averaged between $10 and $12 million per year. Revenues from the 3 percent Hotel and Motel Occupancy Tax have increased from $123,000 in 1995 to nearly $200,000 in 2000 (Natchitoches Parish Tourist Commission 2000a). These revenues serve as the funding basis for marketing efforts by the Natchitoches Parish Tourist Commission. Major marketing activities include an Internet Web site, printed brochures and booklets, and advertisements.

Yet, Natchitoches's concept marketing approach offers benefits beyond the economic impacts of increased tourism and associated revenues. It provides the focus for an entire community's redevelopment, built on a rich culture and historical architectural legacy. Rather than relinquish the past and seek alternative forms of development, Natchitoches has made a commitment to build on its tradition. The combination of culture and historic preservation has worked well for Natchitoches with many positive outcomes for the community and the area.

EUREKA SPRINGS, ARKANSAS
POPULATION: 2,300
CONCEPT: AMERICA'S VICTORIAN VILLAGE

The City That Water Built has a captivating history. From its founding as a source of healing waters leading to boomtown Victorian era development, to recovery from a ghost town of the Great Depression era, Eureka Springs is now a tourist destination. Its strength lies in its history and the preservation of it. Located in the Northwestern Ozark Mountains, only five miles from the Missouri border on Leatherwood Creek, Eureka Spring became one of the most popular health centers in the United States in the late nineteenth century.

Folklore surrounds Eureka Springs. Tribal lore from Native Americans in the area holds that for over 400 years, visits were made to the "magic healing springs" (White 1998:1). Ponce de Leon was reputed to have discovered the springs and was convinced he had discovered the Fountain of Youth. In 1856, Dr. Alvah Jackson and his hunting companions came across the springs and realized that it was the mystical "magic healing waters of the ancient Indians" (White 1998:6). Dr. Jackson's son developed an eye inflammation during the trip and bathed his eyes in the springs. To everyone's surprise, the inflammation cleared and the healing powers of the springs' waters was confirmed (White 1998:7). During the Civil War, a rudimentary hospital was constructed at the springs, and the area gained a reputation for the curative effects of its waters. As people journeyed to the area, a town was born and in 1879, was officially named Eureka, after the Greek meaning of the term, "I found it" (Eureka Springs Parks and Recreation Commission 2000).

The town enjoyed instant success as sensational promises and accounts of miracle cures at the springs spread quickly (Bartlette 2000). Growth was rapid and buildings sprang up to accommodate visitors. Spa resort facilities as well as many Victorian-style home were constructed, lending a delightful ambience to the winding streets and hills of the town (Eureka Springs Historical Museum 2000). Waters from the springs were shipped in ceramic containers throughout the United States, further contributing to its reputation and recognition. By the turn of the century, the population was about 20,000 and included many artists, poets, and writers who extolled "the glories of the scenery and the particular camaraderie of the people in poems, stories, photographs and paintings" (White 1998:8).

In the 1880s, Eureka Springs entered its building boom era. The following excerpts from the historical narrative for the Eureka Springs Survey presented to the National Register of Historic Places illustrates the type of development that occurred:

The economy of Eureka Springs developed around the springs. The springs brought in tourists as well as people with health afflictions with the result that profitable business of hotels, saloons, bathhouses, dry goods stores, groceries and liveries sprang up. The attractions of the springs also brought the investors and the railroad. During this time the Eureka Springs Improvement Company (E.S.I.C.) had a major influence on the development of Eureka Springs and its built environment. The company, organized in 1882 by former Arkansas governor Powell Clayton and other enterprising investors, reflects Eureka Springs' most illustrious period, the "era of big promoters." These men invested heavily in the development and promotion of Eureka Springs as a health center and a retirement place for the wealthy. During this era, 1880–1890, Eureka Springs reached its peak in popularity, wealth and gracious living. . . . Most of the early housing was poorly constructed with no stone or cement foundations. The E.S.I.C. encouraged and erected more substantial buildings. Brick and stone, particularly limestone, sandstone, granite and marble quarried form the surrounding vicinity, were now included in the construction fabric. The company also encouraged the widening of the streets, the installation of street lights, water and sewer systems and wooden sidewalks. Granite and limestone walls were used to terrace the hillsides for construction and landscaping. (U.S. Department of Interior 1980:1–2)

The result was development of lasting Victorian architecture, interwoven among the hills and spring sites. Its hilly topography and scenic setting in the Ozark Mountains has always been appealing. This aesthetic setting, coupled with its historic buildings, provide Eureka Springs with its community economic development foundation.

Impetus for Change

Eureka Springs grew to a population of over 20,000 (Eureka Springs Parks and Recreation Commission 2000) at its apex, around 1900. A decline in its popularity was prompted by several factors: The advent of modern medicine and advances in sciences led to a reduction in faith in the curative powers of the springs, and the St. Louis and North Arkansas Railroad moved its shops out of Eureka Springs to Harrison in the east, lessening Eureka Springs' importance as a commercial center (U.S. Department of Interior 1980:2). By this time, many of the springs had been contaminated by the sewage system put into place in 1894 (White 1998), and the appeal of the town began to diminish.

The year 1908 marks the end of the health spa era, when the luxurious Crescent Hotel became the Crescent College for Girls (U.S. Department of Interior 1980:2). Little new construction took place after this time, and many wooden structures were dismantled and the lumber sold. Eureka Springs weathered both World Wars I and II, and the Great Depression, with little changes in its depressed economy. The most positive outcome of this period was that Eureka Springs' historic structures have remained virtually untouched and intact since the 1890s.

It was not until the late 1950s and early 1960s that interest in Eureka Springs began to resurface. Artists, writers, and retirees began to purchase and refurbish the historic structures in the town. As more people discovered its old-fashioned charm, more tourists visited the area. Thus, after a lapse of nearly sixty years, Eureka Springs entered its second growth phase (Bartlette 2000). This time, the leadership and citizenry of Eureka Springs wanted to structure development for sustainable growth.

Developing the Concept

As with many communities that possess historic buildings, Eureka Springs wanted to protect its resources from encroachment of new development. In 1970, the community created the Eureka Springs Planning Commission to zone districts either Historic Commercial or Historic Residential and to implement ordinances setting design standards to preserve the predominant architectural atmosphere (U.S. Department of Interior 1980). Implementing protective planning measures helped protect Eureka Springs' assets. The community wanted to protect its resources even more, and in 1980, the community applied for and received approval to list its entire downtown in the National Register of Historic Places.

This crucial first step—protecting resources—was taken jointly by the city and the Eureka Springs Chamber of Commerce. As interest in Eureka Springs was renewed, the community leadership realized that its past and its natural resources (the springs and its location in the Ozark Mountains), provided the basis for development of a concept to market the area. Thus, the realization that Eureka Springs could be marketed as America's Victorian Village dawned and serious efforts started to rebuild this identity.

In the 1970s, the City of Eureka Springs formed the Advertising and Promotion Commission to provide marketing services. A special tax was levied on restaurants, hotels, and motels to fund marketing efforts. Along with the Eureka Springs Chamber of Commerce, this group helped market the area as a tourist destination. The Chamber of Commerce has continued marketing efforts and provides assistance with promoting the area as both a retirement community and a tourist destination.

Another partner in the community's redevelopment efforts has been the Eureka Springs Parks and Recreation Commission. Created in 1981, this commission has focused on restoring, improving, and maintaining the resource that prompted the development of Eureka Springs initially, its springs. There are over twenty springs in the city's park system, making it one of the largest municipal park systems in the world (Eureka Springs Parks and Recreation Commission 2000). Springs literally are everywhere in the town, sometimes in combination with caves. Crescent Springs with its Victorian gazebo and the pavilion at Magnetic Springs are just two of the many attractive features of the park system weaving its way throughout the community. Festivals, fairs, and special events are held throughout the year at the springs and parks, providing further use of these natural resources. Tours of the springs and the surrounding areas are offered with various artistic productions and celebrations.

The process of developing the America's Victorian Village concept marketing approach has thus been a joint effort. Using the natural resource base of the mountains and springs, the community has been able to recapture some of its former glory as a tourist and retirement community destination.

Outcomes

Perhaps the most remarkable outcome of Eureka Springs' community concept marketing approach has been its success with tourism. The tourist population is easily double the resident population of only 2,300 on any given night during the peak season. All total, over 1.2 million visitors frequent Eureka Springs on an annual basis.

Because the architecture was literally frozen in time for most of the twentieth century, Eureka Springs possesses a major resource in the form of its historic buildings. These properties have formed the basis for a major historic preservation and restoration efforts, leading to an authentic Victorian-era ambience. Some of these properties now serve the tourism industry, in the form of health spas, hotels, bed and breakfast inns, restaurants, and retail establishments. Over 200 gift shops, craft and antique stores, boutiques, and artists' galleries are now housed in Eureka Springs. Additionally, the architecture serves as the foundation for special events, such as winter holiday tours of Victorian homes. Coupled with the Great Passion Play that runs from May through October, the tourist season has been extended significantly throughout the year (Nelson 1991).

There are over 3,000 lodging rooms in Eureka Springs and more than 70 restaurants (Eureka Springs Chamber of Commerce 1996). Additionally, evening entertainment is offered that has a capacity of over 8,000 guests. Other outcomes as reported by the Eureka Springs Chamber of Commerce and the Arkansas Department of Parks and Tourism include: Nearly 300,000 visitors are greeted on an annual basis at the Visitor Information Center staffed by the Eureka Springs Chamber of Commerce; approximately 200,000 inquiries will be answered by the Chamber of Commerce; more than 3,000 tour groups will visit annually; and over 425,000 passengers will use the trolleys and trams of the Eureka Springs Transit System (Eureka Springs Chamber of Commerce 1996:1).

The growth in tourism is evidenced by the increase in the special tax first levied in 1975 on hotels, motels, and restaurants. With $34,000 collected in 1975, revenues have grown to over $500,000 annually. This enables intense marketing efforts to be conducted on a national level to promote recognition of Eureka Springs' attractiveness.

Dealing with an influx of visitors 500 times the size of the resident population, Eureka Springs has done a remarkable job of promoting and maintaining their tourism industry. Their concept marketing approach has been extremely successful, with an economy resurrected from ghost town status. Building on its history and its natural resources, Eureka Springs has won the upper hand in the community redevelopment game.

ETHNICITY

Ethnic links can serve as a powerful basis on which to build a concept marketing approach. The following three communities illustrate the ability to preserve ethnic ties while addressing community economic development needs. Fredericksburg, Texas; Solvang, California; and New Glarus, Wisconsin, all have strong ethnic bases that serve as the basis on which to build community concept marketing approaches.

FREDERICKSBURG, TEXAS
POPULATION: 7,944
CONCEPT: FREDERICKSBURG IN THE TEXAS HILL COUNTRY,
AN ENDURING HERITAGE

In 1846, a group of German immigrants seeking a better quality of life, one free from religious and political oppression, settled deep in the heart of Texas Hill Country, in a town they named Fredericksburg, after the German nobleman, Prince Frederick of Prussia. Within a few short years, it was considered a progressive and successful community. Under the leadership of John O. Meusebach, a German baron, a treaty was signed with the Native American Comanche tribe, and the treaty was never broken.

The distinctiveness of the German culture and ethnic links are apparent in Fredericksburg, yet it was the dedication to concepts of freedom and education that prevailed in the community. This excerpt from a document compiled by the Gillespie County Historical Society and Commission illustrates these ideals:

Determined not to give up their religious faiths and equally determined that their children should have an education, one of the first buildings constructed by the pioneers in Fredericksburg was the Vereins Kirche. This building, placed in the middle of Main Street, was to serve as a church, school, community hall and fortress.... The laying of the cornerstone in 1847 was a great event. This occurred one month after the famous peace treaty between Meusebach and the Indians. They had promised presents on the next full moon, and arrived in Fredericksburg on this day in their best, most colorful attire. The mingling of the settlers and the Indians on this memorable occasion perhaps did much to make the peace treaty one of the most famous and most binding in American History. (Gillespie County Historical Society and Commission 1981:2)

The commitment to a progressive society that permeates the ethos of Fredericksburg today. *Gemutlichkeit*, the German word for a friendly and comfortable environment, described Fredericksburg in its early days (Fredericksburg Chamber of Commerce 2000). It still exudes this charm as well as the warmth of a small town German environment.

The ethnic ties to Germany also have been expressed in the arts. Most of the settlers were well educated in the liberal arts, with a strong emphasis on music and theater (Convention and Visitors Bureau of Fredericksburg Texas 2000). It is speculated that the arts provided another venue for expression of political and social views; whether or not this is true, the citizens of Fredericksburg were producing operas and dramas as early as 1850 (Convention and Visitors Bureau of Fredericksburg Texas 2000:1). The dedication to the arts still permeates the community today, and was noted in the 1990s as one of the best small art towns in America (Convention and Visitors Bureau of Fredericksburg Texas 2000:1). The focus on the arts has provided an attraction for tourists as well as quality entertainment for its citizens.

Located equidistant from Austin and San Antonio, Fredericksburg was a sleepy small agricultural town until a railroad connected it with San Antonio after the turn of the twentieth century. The town prospered as an agricultural center, with several wineries being established. The area is also noted for its peaches and wildflowers, both leading to related industries. A variety of other industries are located in the area too, from a musical instrument manufacturer to machined parts production (Fredericksburg Chamber of Commerce 2000). The economy is diversified with its agricultural, industrial, service, and tourism-related businesses.

Impetus for Change

Fredericksburg is rather unique in the sense that there was not a catalyzing event or major decline in the economy that prompted its investigation of a concept marketing approach. Rather, the attributes and attractiveness of the town became apparent as national attention focused on the home of Admiral Nimitz and the Naval Museum, which now includes the George Bush Gallery of the Pacific War. Admiral Nimitz's grandfather established the Nimitz Hotel, which in earlier times hosted many famous travelers. It gained significant national attention when Lyndon Johnson, who had a ranch in Fredericksburg, became president of the United States.

Given its rather diverse economy, Fredericksburg had other choices for economic development. Yet, the ability to showcase its German ethnic ties and historical features provided an appealing approach for further diversifying the economy.

Developing the Concept

Tourists trickled in after the publicity provided for Fredericksburg during the Johnson administration, but it was not until the late 1970s and early 1980s that tourism gained momentum. At this point, the local civic leadership realized that the community's German ethnic roots could be used to build recognition of Fredericksburg as a tourist destination (Kammlah 2000). The local chamber and other organizations established the fall Octoberfest, attracting many visitors from San Antonio, Austin, and other cities. Tourism began to really accelerate as more people realized the charm of the small town in the Texas Hill Country.

The chamber of commerce and the convention and visitors bureau began marketing Fredericksburg aggressively. While the chamber of commerce focuses on a variety of economic development activities, the bureau focuses on tourism development. With funds of nearly $500,000 received from the special tax levied on lodging establishments, the Convention and Visitors Bureau provides services for national and international marketing activities. Recently, efforts have begun to market Fredericksburg to European visitors.

The Gillespie County Historical Society founded in 1934 also helps promote Fredericksburg as a tourist venue by preserving its heritage and ethnic links. It operates two museums, the Vereins Kirche and the Pioneer Complex. Its also sponsors the annual Founders Festival to commemorate the founding of the city, two public lecture programs a year, the Christmas Candlelight Tour, and a summer social (Gillespie County Historical Society and Commission 2000).

The German ethnic links are not the only focus of marketing efforts. Since they are located in the Texas Hill Country, the cowboy and western themes are marketing activities too. Fredericksburg has not re-created themselves in a façade of German heritage (Kammlah 2000). Instead of promoting the German ethnicity exclusively, they regard it as part of their way of life. Yet, even without the strong promotion of its ethnicity, Fredericksburg is recognized as providing visitors with a genuine German ethnic experience, Texas Hill Country style.

Outcomes

Tourism has been a major success for Fredericksburg, which is now consistently rated as one of the top fifteen tourist attractions in Texas (Kammlah 2000). Over a million tourists now visit Fredericksburg, which is noted for a festival or special event nearly every weekend. There are more than 80 historic sites, 120 shops and stores, 50 restaurants, and nearby recreational activities to attract visitors (Convention and Visitors Bureau of Fredericksburg Texas 2000).

The outcomes are impressive: Tourism has encouraged the commercial use of historical properties, including homes that have been converted into bed and breakfast inns or guest houses. Coupled with new construction, Fredericksburg offers over 300 of these inns or guest houses, along with 500 motel rooms. The lodging tax has increased steadily every year during the 1990s, as have sales tax revenues. In 1991, $186,000 were collected for the lodging tax; in 1998 this had increased to $603,000. Sales tax revenue increases are equally impressive, growing from $1.7 million in 1995 to $2.3 million in 1999 (Fredericksburg Chamber of Commerce 2000).

Fredericksburg has indeed succeeded in its concept marketing efforts. Incorporating its German ethnic traditions, the community has implemented an effective development strategy of tourism in the Texas Hill Country.

SOLVANG, CALIFORNIA
POPULATION: 5,125
CONCEPT: DANISH CAPITAL OF AMERICA

The Danes arrived in the Santa Ynez Valley with a mission: establish a Danish-American colony with a folk school to preserve the culture of Danish immigrants. In 1911, Danish settlers from Iowa and Michigan traveled west to the valley, located fifteen miles west of the Pacific Ocean and forty miles north of Santa Barbara (Rife 1978). They purchased land there and named it Solvang, meaning sunny fields in Danish. With sunshine nearly 340 days a year, the name was appropriate.

The overall purpose of Solvang's founding and development was to preserve the Danish culture, in the style of the old world folk schools of Denmark. The philosophy of the school, Atterdag College, permeated early life in Solvang. The three-story wooden structure was literally the center of the community; this account of Atterdag College sums its influence in the community (Rife 1978:10):

There the Danish culture would continue with the idea that education educated for living life, not solely to earn a living. There were no examinations and no degrees. There was a love of life, a love of learning for its own sake. There was the study of history, of composition, of literature, of mathematics. There were debates and drama, gymnastics and "sanglege" (singing-dances). They sang the songs of heroism and daring, or right and courage, of honesty and integrity.

Sadly, Atterdag and its ideals could not compete with American-style schools, and it closed its doors in 1937. Razed in 1970, the spirit of the folk school lives in the festivals and celebrations in Solvang.

Yet, this strong ethnic link of Danish culture has always directed Solvang in its development. It has always been noted as a center for Danish culture and as such, attracted the future Danish King and Queen Frederik IX and Ingrid for a visit in 1939. Danes of worldwide reputation also were attracted to Solvang, with visits and concerts from Victor Borge and Lauritz Melchoir in 1943 (Rife 1978:12).

The Danes built a town out of the bean fields, and often constructed their buildings in Danish style architecture. Although many of the early historic buildings no longer exist, the Danish provincial architectural style permeates the community.

Impetus for Change

The early days of Solvang focused on farming and related agriculture activities. Although the focus of the folk school had diminished, the desire to preserve and promote Danish ethnicity had not. After World War II, several members of the community realized that tourism could provide a way for the farm town to both preserve its ethnic ties and provide economic development activities. Several homes, windmills, and a downtown block of commercial buildings were constructed in the Danish provincial style.

This foray into architecture, along with the Danish Days festival that grew out of Solvang's twenty-fifth anniversary celebration in 1936 (Rife 1978:10), garnered attention as an ethnic venue. An article and accompanying photos highlighting Solvang's Danish Days celebration in a 1946 edition of the *Saturday Evening Post* provided the national attention it needed to become serious about its tourism intentions.

Developing the Concept

Solvang, with its authentic ethnic links, did not have to create a concept. The concept was there in the lifestyle and traditions of the people in the community. What it needed was a focus for further protecting and enhancing these ethnic ties, and the community found this in the form of tourism.

The effort in the early stages of the development of Solvang as the Danish Capital of America was primarily conducted by the private sector. Solvang was not actually a city, rather a town in Santa Barbara County and was not incorporated until the 1980s (Traylor 2000). The local property owners decided to re-create the existing downtown in the Danish style. Dormers, gables, arches, and copper and thatched roofs appeared, and stores began importing Danish products; the arcade in its pastel colors and flowers was transformed into a magical bit of provincial Denmark (Rife 1978:14). Shortly thereafter, members of the Danish royal family visited, prompting more attention to Solvang from its native land of Denmark.

More and more citizens decided to construct new buildings and homes in the Danish provincial style, which added to Solvang's attractiveness to tourists. Coupled with an expanded Danish Days celebration, Solvang was on its way to becoming a significant tourist destination.

After its incorporation, the City of Solvang contracted with the Conference and Visitors Bureau to conduct major marketing efforts. Additional festivals and special events were added, as well as a replica of a 1915 streetcar which is pulled through the heart of town by a pair of Belgian draft horses (Solvang California Conference and Visitors Bureau 2000).

Solvang is uniquely positioned to capitalize on its ethnic ties. Because of the factor of authenticity, it has been a relatively smooth transition for Solvang from farming community to Danish culture mecca for tourists. The Danish culture is pervasive throughout the city, from traditional Danish food, music, Old World arts, and even the tradition of placing a stork on rooftops of homes and shops to bring good luck. Its ethnic links have resulted in what some Danish visitors describe as "more like Denmark than Denmark" (Solvang California Conference and Visitors Bureau 2000:4). This is a reflection of the commitment of the citizens of Solvang to its Danish heritage and ethnic traditions (see Photographs 5.3 and 5.4 for examples of how culture is displayed in Solvang).

Outcomes

Nearly 2 million tourists per year visit Solvang. Amazingly, 50 percent of these visitors are from other countries (Traylor 2000). This is due to several factors: The Conference and Visitors Bureau markets intensively to European and other countries for tourists, as well as making regional and national level efforts in the United States; and Solvang has strong ties to Denmark, a source for tourists as well.

This represents a remarkable transformation from a small farming town to a tourist destination that accommodates many times its population in annual visitors.

Photograph 5.3
Confronting Culture, Solvang, California

Courtesy of Solvang Conference and Visitors Bureau, Solvang, California.

Businesses supporting the tourist industry have emerged, including restaurants, bakeries, art galleries, shops, hotels, motels, and resorts. Attractions such as the Hans Christian Andersen Museum and the Elverhoy Museum of History and Art further promote Danish ethnic links. Myriad festivals and events, such as the Torch Light Parade, along with performances by folk dancers and musicians, draw large crowds.

Through tourism, the City of Solvang is provided with its primary revenue source. Sales tax receipts have steadily increased from the early days of tourism to a level of $819,000 in 1994 to over $944,000 in fiscal year 1999–2000. A special tax levied on hotels, motels, and bed and breakfast inns has increased nearly 20 percent, from $972,000 in 1993 to nearly $1.2 million at the close of the fiscal year in 2000 (City of Solvang 2000). These revenues fund services, infrastructure improvements, and other essential supporting activities. The Conference and Visitors Bureau receives $350,000 in tax revenues annually to market Solvang (Traylor 2000).

Photograph 5.4
Cultural Accouterments, Solvang, California

Courtesy of Solvang Conference and Visitors Bureau, Solvang, California.

Solvang is proud of its heritage and proud of its accomplishment of preserving its Danish ethnicity while providing community economic development activities. Positioning its ethnic links has worked well for Solvang to build a community concept marketing approach.

NEW GLARUS, WISCONSIN
POPULATION: 2,000
CONCEPT: AMERICA'S LITTLE SWITZERLAND

New Glarus is the epitome of a town steeped in ethnicity. It is not an invented ethnic place (Hoelscher 1998) or one that has emerged only in response to economic development pressures. Rather, it is the original version of an enclave of Swiss immigrants who clung steadfastly to their traditions. Continuing expressions of group connectedness in the form of annual commemorations of Swiss Independence, yearly reaffirmations to the church, and decennial celebrations of New Glarus' settlement have remained significant components of New Glarus' public memory for 150 years (Hoelscher 1998:29).

Located 25 miles southwest of Madison and a two-hour drive from Chicago, New Glarus was founded in southern Wisconsin in 1846 by a group of Swiss immigrants who purchased 1,280 acres of land in the Little Sugar River Valley. Having left the canton Glarus in Switzerland and purchased the land with funds from the Glarus Emmigrations Society, the name was a natural choice (Stocker-McLane 1995). The original Glarus was suffering from a lack of jobs and difficult economic times, which provided the impetus for a group of its citizens to seek better opportunities in the United States.

Transitioning from the industry of Glarus to the agriculture-based economy in Wisconsin was difficult at first. Dairy farming became a staple activity, and after a few decades and the arrival of many more Swiss immigrants bringing their heritage of Swiss cheesemaking with them, the settlers had developed New Glarus into one of the centers of the Wisconsin cheese industry by 1880. At its peak in the early 1900s, New Glarus was home to twenty-two cheesemaking factories, including some that produced one of the finest cheese varieties in the United States (Stocker-McLane 1995:55).

The area thus developed on the basis of agriculture and related industries, with the residents maintaining strong ties to their Swiss heritage. Ethnicity has been, and remains, a vital component of the community of New Glarus. As Hoelscher (1998:29) describes in his book, *Heritage on Stage*, "The notion that the small ethnic enclave possessed a past worthy of commemoration occurred to the Swiss colony shortly after establishing its New World base. To a most remarkable degree, that idea persists to this day." This commitment to its ethnic traditions has provided New Glarus with its concept marketing foundation.

Impetus for Change

The dairy farming industry and related activities, including the production of condensed milk and other products, kept the New Glarus economy relatively stable until the early 1960s. At that time, the Pet Milk Factory closed, negatively impacting the stable economic base of the community (Schiesser 2000). The cheesemaking industry had also declined from its peak earlier in the twentieth century. Although cheesemaking remains a vital component of the New Glarus area, it is no longer the mainstay of the economy.

As agriculture and industry declined, it was apparent to New Glarus' residents that a new economic activity was needed to foster stability. Several festivals and special events that the residents of New Glarus used to celebrate their Swiss heritage, such as the William Tell drama, the Heidi Festival, and the commemoration of Swiss Independence Day, provided a basis on which to build an expanded economic activity: tourism.

Developing the Concept

Different organizations sponsored and produced the various festivals and special events. In the 1970s, the organizations collaborated to form the New Glarus Tourism Advertising Program, pulling together a variety of resources and groups (Schiesser 2000). At its inception, the program was purely a volunteer effort.

New Glarus possessed a valuable resource on which to build tourism-based activities: its heritage and ethnicity. Helping to preserve this heritage is the New Glarus Historical Society, formed in 1938 for the purpose of preserving the history, records, and material artifacts of New Glarus. The society owns and operates the Swiss Historical Village, a museum with fourteen buildings representing life in New Glarus in the nineteenth century. Included are a replica of a cheese factory, a traditional Swiss bee house, a smoke house, a print shop, and traditional log buildings (New Glarus Historical Society 2000). The Swiss Historical Village and the New Glarus Historical Society provided a venue for helping to develop tourism activities.

The concept of New Glarus as America's Little Switzerland was a natural fit, due to its strong and pervasive ethnic links. The architectural style prior to the 1970s was not necessarily Swiss; indeed, the town early in the twentieth century had taken on the appearance of other small American towns. Yet, it was the sense of ethnicity and the reverence for Swiss values and customs that made New Glarus different from the other towns. There were a few notable exceptions, such as the New Glarus Hotel built in 1853 and the Chalet of the Golden Fleece, built in 1937 by the founder of the Wilhelm Tell drama (Hoelscher 1998).

In the 1970s, several property owners decided to re-create their buildings in traditional Swiss chalet design. Interestingly, not one chalet exists in the canton of Glarus; rather, the architectural style reflects that of the Bernese mountain area in Switzerland (Stocker-McLane 1995:53). Thus, the town of New Glarus borrowed the Swiss chalet style to complement its ethnic traditions. In this sense, New Glarus's atmosphere is artificial, yet few other places could claim more of a right to importing Swiss architectural style than can New Glarus. The New Glarus Chamber of Commerce describes the architectural style:

The Bernese Mountain Chalet is the most widely recognized Swiss design. It is characterized by its white plaster foundation, brown stained wood walls, geranium-filled flower boxes, and intricately detailed woodwork in the chalet interior. Notable examples of this style include The Chalet of the Golden Fleece museum and the New Glarus Hotel. The Chalet Landhaus and the Schoco-Laden are contemporary examples of the Bernese style. The Kubly home shows the sweeping roof lines and curved fascia characteristics of the Swiss Emmental Style. The Swiss Valley Orchard barn is a contemporary example of the Emmental style of architecture. Other contemporary designs include the Bank of New Glarus, the New Glarus Village Hall, Anderson's Kaufhaus and the Amcore Bank. Ruef's Meat Market, Robert's and other merchants renovated storefronts to complement the Swiss/European ambiance of the village. (New Glarus Chamber of Commerce 2000:3)

Marketing efforts have paid off, and New Glarus has gained a reputation nationally and internationally, as a tourist destination. Revenues collected from advertisements placed in printed marketing publications fund not only the materials, but also the visitor information booth (Schiesser 2000).

Most of the efforts to develop the marketing concept have been made by the private and nonprofit sectors. With organizations sponsoring festivals and special events, and the private sector providing the properties constructed or renovated in the Swiss provincial style New Glarus has emerged as a tourist destination. Intent on preserving this style of development, the public leadership has recently passed a planning and design ordinance to establish standards of development (see Photograph 5.5 for an example of the Swiss provincial-style architecture).

Outcomes

The ability of New Glarus to parlay its ethnicity into a tourism development strategy is impressive. It has been exceedingly well received in the cultural and heritage tourism industry, due in large measure to its authentic heritage and history. It is not a created village, it is a reflection of the strong heritage of the Swiss settlers.

Perhaps the most recognized event is the Wilhelm Tell Festival, in which the drama is performed several times over the Labor Day weekend, both in German and English. Including a cast of nearly 200 and a variety of livestock, the drama has been re-enacted for over fifty years (Tritt 1999). The event draws thousands of visitors each year to partake in the events and enjoy the spectacular event.

New Glarus is virtually a year-round tourist destination now, with a variety of events and festivals taking place in each season. The Heidi Festival is held in June of each year and draws several thousand visitors. In May, the Swiss Polkafest provides dancing activities. Fall brings various events focused on harvest themes; Christmas and the winter season feature a variety of activities as well.

The impact of the concept marketing approach for New Glarus has been positive. While official counts are not held of the volumes of tourists, it is estimated that many thousands of people visit each year. This success is reflected in the viability of New Glarus's business community, including hotels, bed and breakfast inns, restaurants, shops, and attractions. Visitors from Switzerland frequent New Glarus and are fascinated by the dedication to preservation of the Old World Swiss culture and heritage. The appeal of New Glarus's Old World village charm is apparent. Indeed, the guest book of the Swiss Historical Village indicates visitors from every state in the United States, as well as many foreign countries. New Glarus is pleased with its efforts to preserve its heritage and achieve economic development goals, building on the tradition of ethnicity.

SUMMARY

Building on tradition is the idea of utilizing and enhancing existing historic or ethnic resources to develop a concept marketing approach and achieve community revitalization. The six profiles presented in this chapter illustrate how communities can incorporate their historic or ethnic resources to enable effective community concept marketing. Each is unique and approached the identification, design, and implementation of its concept marketing approach in different manners. Yet, each is successful and reaps the benefits of its efforts for community economic development.

Photograph 5.5
Ethnicity in Design, New Glarus, Wisconsin

Courtesy of New Glarus Chamber of Commerce, New Glarus, Wisconsin.

Several findings of this research hold relevance to others desiring to construct and implement a community concept marketing approach. While the approaches to constructing the concept vary, it is crucial that a valid link be present in order to effectively build on a tradition of historic or ethnic resources. For a concept built on historic preservation, questions to ask include the following:

- Are there historic structures (commercial, residential, or other) in the community?
- Are the existing structures targets for restoration or re-creation?
- Is there interest from the private sector in funding restoration efforts? If not, are funds available via the public or nonprofit sectors?

For community concept marketing efforts based on ethnicity, it is vital to ask questions like the following:

- Does the community have an ethnic link to preserve or enhance?
- Is the link valid?
- Will developing this link be acceptable to the community?
- Are there organizations, such as historical societies? If not, can one be formed to help identify the link's history?
- To which groups will the ethnic link have appeal?

There are many other aspects to consider before embarking on development of a traditional or ethnic community concept approach. These include the following factors and questions:

- Are the overall goals of the community conducive to support either historic preservation efforts or ethnicity-based development?
- Is there a champion in the community—civic organization, community group, business interest, public sector leader—who will lead the efforts to design and implement such a concept marketing approach?
- Is there interest in such community economic development expressed by all three sectors—the public sector, at the local, state, or national levels; the private sector business community; and the nonprofit or civic sector?
- How will funding be obtained? The majority of communities impose a special tax levied to collect funds for supporting marketing and improvements in the community's infrastructure.
- Is there a commitment by local government to implement supportive ordinances, such as design standards or zoning regulations, to protect the historic resources of the community?
- Finally, will the consequences of implementing a traditional or ethnic community concept marketing approach be desirable? There are often unintended consequences that citizens may find difficult to live with, such as intense traffic congestion or intrusion into "community spaces."

6

Creating the Surrealistic

The image of cities and communities can be a great asset, or hindrance, to community economic development and the development of marketing concepts. Crilley (1993:231–233) in "Architecture as Advertising: Constructing the Image of Redevelopment" makes this point clearly:

The postmodern architecture of redevelopment—with its facadal displays, penchant for recycling imagery and theoretical rationale in semiotic theory—is fully incorporated into the ideological apparatus of place marketing, playing a major role in mediating perceptions of urban change and persuading "us" of the virtues and cultural beneficence of speculative investments. . . . Architecture has once again become a form of advertising as governments, powerful corporations and innumerable redevelopment agencies show a renewed interest in manipulating the built environment pro-actively.

Some communities have taken the idea of building an image to a different plane altogether: surrealism, or the "principles, ideals, or practice of producing fantastic or incongruous imagery or effects in art, literature, film, or theater by means of unnatural juxtapositions and combinations" (Merriam-Webster, Inc. 1988:1188). Applying this definition to community economic development implies the use of imagery or other effects that induce a dreamlike atmosphere. This type of concept marketing approach is of an incongruous nature that defies or exceeds common expectations. Certainly, history or other basis of reality can serve as the foundation for the concept, yet application usually goes beyond what would be expected.

What then, exactly, is the surreal community concept marketing approach? To further expand and apply this definition to community concept marketing, surrealism is the juxtaposition of elements within a community to create, or re-create, a new environment. In other words, a community can literally create a concept that has no historical or cultural basis, and with proper application, sell itself as this new entity. Just as people are expounded to re-create themselves, thanks to the self-help movement of several decades, communities can be re-created as well.

FASCINATION WITH IMITATION

Concept approaches based on surrealism can have a high level of market appeal. In the United States, there is a long history of fascination with imitation. In the Victorian era, the nation became fascinated with lifelike reproductions and re-creations, and was even referred to as the "culture of imitation" (Curtis 2000:35). This fascination was reflected in many activities, including the re-creation of the White City (Grecian and Roman buildings) at the 1893 World's Colombian Exposition in Chicago—this event launched the City Beautiful Movement that spurred construction of neo-Classical public buildings throughout the United States (Levy 1997). The fascination with imitation has not ceased. Pendleton, Indiana (population 2,000) found this fascination plays well in their community. To kick off the holiday season each year just before Thanksgiving, fake snow—shredded Styrofoam—is spread throughout the shopping district and attracts thousands of visitors (Hageman 2000). Perhaps it goes beyond mere fascination—Americans have been characterized as being *addicted* to fantasy and simulation (Curtis 2000:35), and with good cause. This bodes well for communities desiring to develop a concept marketing applications based on surrealism.

ELEMENTS OF SURREALISM

Building the surreal environment takes creativity as well as boldness and, in some cases, audaciousness. The willingness of a community to develop, implement, and market on this basis implies a serious desire to re-create a community. In many cases, it is a matter of survival. For others, it is a matter of economic diversification. There are numerous ways that a community can develop a concept marketing approach based on surrealism. One of the major components is *shock value*. Is it completely unnatural to the point that it does not attract visitors? If this is the case, it can go too far and not be successful, as was the case with a community in Kansas that tried to develop a re-creation of a Polynesian village. Somehow, the Polynesian ambience could not be achieved with cornfields surrounding the site.

Without a doubt, the ultimate example of the mastery of surrealism as a concept marketing approach in the United States is Las Vegas. There, incongruity is exemplified. The creation of Las Vegas is truly remarkable, given its isolated location and its lack of water and other natural resources. Located in a desert, Las Vegas literally was created as an entertainment capital. Originally based on gambling, the large casinos of the past are being replaced by even more incongruent attractions. Entertainment facilities include shopping, dining, and other activities that look like streets of Paris, a Moroccan bazaar, or the canals of Venice. A replica of the Great Pyramid of Egypt confronts the visitor, and larger than life pirate ships battle in a harbor. Easily one of the most incongruent locations on earth to host such activities, Las Vegas is the epitome of a surrealistic approach and certainly wins in the category of shock value. It has been described as a "grand train wreck of geography and cultures and epochs" and the site where the experience of place has been replaced by place of experience (Curtis 2000:34). By creating an artificial environment in a pleasing manner, Las Vegas captures the benefits of catering to cultural fascination by using imagery, theming, and fantasy.

Not a community, but certainly larger than any community discussed in this book is another master of surrealism, the Disney Company. Noted for it ability to create dreamlike environments, Disney has re-created numerous themes throughout its properties. Their approach is partly based on *scale*—the ability to develop the created environment to a plausible level. Scale has relevance to communities attempting to create a concept marketing approach too: Is there enough to create the environment? One street of a created concept may not be enough to pull in visitors. At the same time, few communities have the resources to finance a large-scale creation. Ririe, Idaho (population 596), with a sign welcoming visitors that reads, "You just thought you were lost. You're in Ririe, Idaho," attempted to develop a large-scale surreal concept (Richards 1996). Estimated to cost over $10 million, Ririe wanted to create a Space Discovery Station on a potato field. The idea was to use NASA surplus equipment to create a spacelike environment to attract tourists. Although NASA donated various surplus equipment to Ririe, including a simulator, the community was not able to raise the funds to finance a project of this scale.

Shock value and scale are not the only elements of surrealistic concept marketing approaches. The *scope* of the concept is vital too. By scope, it is meant that communities must find a concept that incorporates activities and venues appealing to a market. Sometimes the scope is found in response to interests expressed by the public. For example, the interest in mysticism provides several communities with the basis for development of a concept marketing approach. Tiny Calistoga, Florida, has found that its reputation as a center for providing palm readings and other psychic services has accelerated visits by tourists. Curious to see and experience the unusual in Calistoga, visitors can also enjoy eating in one of the cafes or staying in the renovated historic hotel in town that have sprung up to serve them. Mysticism has long held attraction for certain tourist markets, as evidenced by the continued interest in the Sedona, Arizona, area and other venues that provide glimpses of something spiritual or mystical.

THE SURREAL

Communities can literally create a concept for which there is no precedent with energy and imagination. The following communities exemplify this approach, which incorporate elements of incongruity and in some cases, unnatural juxtaposition, with notable results. Mount Dora, Florida; Helen, Georgia; Holland, Michigan; Roswell, New Mexico; and Valentine, Nebraska have all succeeded in developing a community concept marketing approach containing varying degrees of surrealism. Mount Dora has used its architecture to produce the ambience of a New England town in South Florida; Helen has shaped a Bavarian village from its mountainous North Georgia location; Holland has built on its Dutch ties to create a genuine atmosphere complete with historical structures relocated from the Netherlands; Roswell has captured the realm of outer world experiences; and Valentine has endeared itself with activities that reflect the holiday that shares its name. In all but one of these communities, some event or historical tie inspired the selection of their particular concept application.

MOUNT DORA, FLORIDA
POPULATION: 9,200
CONCEPT: THE NEW ENGLAND OF THE SOUTH

Located in Central Florida, Mount Dora is an "anomaly in every sense of the word" (Mount Dora Area Chamber of Commerce 2000). Located twenty-seven miles northwest of Orlando on a hilltop overlooking Lake Dora, it qualifies as Florida's only mountaintop town at an elevation of 184 feet above sea level. Yet, it is the architectural style of the city that sets it apart from every other in the state: it is distinctly New England. As such, it is an unusual Florida setting and attracts visitors and new residents alike. It is an example of how the elements of shock value (incongruity) and scale have been utilized to build the concept marketing approach.

How did Mount Dora come to be this way? Established in 1880, it had only a handful of settlers, some of whom relocated from New England. In 1887, the first railroad service was established and gradually increased to two passenger trains per day by 1915, bringing visitors from larger cities in Florida to Lake Dora. Because of the number of lakes in the area, tourists could travel to Mount Dora via steamboat. With the building of the Lakeside Inn in 1882 and the later expansion of the complex in the early 1900s, Mount Dora became an even more desirable destination. With more expansions in the 1920s, the dedication was overseen by former President Calvin Coolidge and the appeal of the Great Gatsby era town grew (Mount Dora Area Chamber of Commerce 1999). The Lakeside Inn is now listed on the National Register of Historic Places and is one of only five Florida lodges that has been designated a Historic Hotel of America by the Trust for Historic Preservation.

Other properties built in the style of New England architecture are now considered historic treasures: the Donnelly House built by a former resident of Pittsburgh, Pennsylvania; the Mount Dora Depot; and the Mount Dora City Hall built in the 1880s.

Selecting the Concept

Mount Dora's economic base was citrus, although tourism grew as well due to its physical beauty and the lakes. The concept was self-selected in the sense that it became a re-creation of a New England town because the citizens built in that style. Fortunately, Mount Dora never experienced the crushing population growth of other Florida towns and much of the ambience and historic architecture has been preserved. The city has used this existing resource to further maintain its unique style and charm which is certainly atypical of Florida communities. It was not until the 1990s that the city began to capitalize on this concept to market the area to visitors, industry, and new residents.

Developing the Concept

Mount Dora did not progress through the usual process of identifying and developing, or re-creating a concept for community marketing. Rather, they inherited the concept, based on how the town was built historically and by preserving its charm through the decades. In the 1990s, it became apparent that the town itself could serve as the basis for further marketing and quality growth. The City of Mount Dora then implemented a historic preservation ordinance to protect the built assets and appointed a Historic Preservation Board comprised of a group of citizens appointed by the mayor (City of Mount Dora 1997). This board reviews all requests for renovation and any related work on historic properties.

Further, the city developed and maintains nine parks that serve as venues for not only re-creation but also special events and festivities. Palm Island Park has a nature education focus, and nearby Simpson Cove and Grantham Point are home to the only inland freshwater lighthouse in Florida. Evans Park is home to the annual lawn bowling tournament; Mount Dora is home to the second largest lawn bowling club in the United States (Fox 2000). Historic Donnelly Park hosts concerts and other events and is located in the central park of historic downtown.

A variety of festivals, theatre, and special events have been designed to increase tourism to Mount Dora. Some have endured from earlier days, such as the Mount Dora Theatre Company, which has been giving performances since 1948 and is now located in the historic Ice House building. The April Spring Festival, a celebration of music and literature also draws visitors, as well as the annual Fine Arts Festival.

The efforts to preserve and enhance Mount Dora have been community wide. The private sector helps sponsor events and has formed the Village Merchants Association to advertise and market Mount Dora. The chamber of commerce is committed to preserving the ambience of the city and focuses its attention on supportive activities such as recruiting retirees to locate there. The city supports preservation with ordinances and regulations, as well as supporting infrastructure.

Outcomes

Mount Dora has become nationally recognized for its uniqueness as a New England town in the South. In 1994 and again in 1997 it was named one of the best places to retire and also is listed as one of the 100 Great Towns in America (Willis 2001). With that recognition has come more growth. In the period 1980 to 1990,

Mount Dora experienced an 11 percent increase in population, from 6,483 residents to 7,196 (Fox 2000). With population approaching 10,000 in the year 2000, Mount Dora has experienced nearly a 25 percent increase in population in the period 1990–2000. Retirees account for many of the newcomers, although young families are attracted to the affordable housing compared to Orlando and other urban areas in Florida.

The Fine Arts Festival impacts the city greatly. Each year, it attracts about 300,000 visitors—a large influx for a community with less than 10,000 residents. The Antique Boat Festival brings in about 75,000 visitors, and the Craft Fair attracts over 200,000. With over half a million visitors, Mount Dora has had to respond with supporting infrastructure and considerations for impact on the existing assets of the city.

The efforts to build on the already existing basis as a concept has been successful for Mount Dora. Tourism has increased dramatically and new residents are attracted to its charm and ambience. Although incongruent at first glance, Mount Dora has succeeded in transporting an architectural style of another region and capturing the benefits of this concept.

HELEN, GEORGIA
POPULATION: 430
CONCEPT: ALPINE VILLAGE

Only 1.5 miles long, Helen is located in the North Georgia Mountains on the Chattahoochee River. Within its borders is something fairly astounding: a recreation of an Alpine village, complete with cobblestone alleys and gabled roofs. This unique village attracts millions of visitors each year with its close proximity to two urban centers, Atlanta and Greenville, South Carolina. It is one of the best examples of a community that has incorporated all elements of a surrealistic concept marketing approach—scale, scope, and shock value (incongruity).

Helen has a rich history. The area formerly served as the major ceremonial and trading center of the Cherokee Nation. Major trading routes were established that later formed the basis of Interstate 75. With the Trail of Tears, the Cherokee were relocated to reservations in the Western United States despite the firmly established communities in the region. Although settlers of European ancestry were already in the area, the relocation of the Cherokee Nation opened up the area for more settlers and the valley experienced an influx of population. During the Great Georgia Gold Rush, thousands of miners flooded into the valley, and the area prospered. The reserves were quickly exhausted and by the end of the 1800s, the mines were no longer productive. Later, timber companies were attracted to the area by the large virgin forests. When the Gainesville and Northwestern Railroad followed along the Chattahoochee River and established service in the valley in 1913, a station was built in the village. Named Helen, after a daughter of a railroad surveyor, the town thrived with sawmill operations and other lumber industry enterprises (Alpine Helen/White County Convention and Visitors Bureau 2000).

Selecting the Concept

As with gold, the timber supplies in the area were quickly exhausted, and in the 1930s, the lumber industries were ceasing operations (Alpine Helen/White County Convention and Visitors Bureau 2000:5). With all the timber cut, no gold, and little prospects of other industrial activities, the village of Helen did not have a bright future. It continued to survive until the 1960s, when only six businesses remained in a dreary row of concrete block structures.

There did not seem to be much hope for survival of the small mountain village until four local business owners met to talk about options for the future in 1968. They decided to create something new and different that would attract tourists from Atlanta and other urban centers. At that point, they approached an artist from the region, John Kollock, who had been stationed in Europe during World War II (Brack 1994). Asking him about suggestions for painting or decorating the buildings in the village spurred his creation of the Alpine Village concept. Mr. Kollock recalled the lovely Bavarian villages he had seen during his war service and he composed renderings of Helen with facades, gables, and rooftops in this architectural style. In January of 1969, the business owners decided they had little to lose and eagerly began a re-creation of their buildings in the Bavarian style (McCall 2000). The visual appeal of the village was not high before this process began, as evidenced in Photograph 6.1. Within several years, however, the visual appeal had improved dramatically, as shown in the Photograph 6.2.

Developing the Concept

The effort to develop the concept has been a private sector initiative. The buildings were renovated by private owners, and this approach has been adhered to since that time. The village government provides support for the concept and has established a set of architectural guidelines and design standards to ensure that the buildings comply with the theme (Morgan 2000). Any new building or renovation must comply with a series of design standards, including selection of certain paint colors, window shapes, dormers, gables, and other features of Bavarian village architecture. These regulations protect the basis of the concept marketing approach—the visual impact of an Alpine village in North Georgia. Additional support for infrastructure improvements has been made as well to support the increased volume of visitors and traffic to the village.

One of the four business owners who originally helped develop the concept of Alpine Helen decided to copy a ceremony from Munich, Germany. Held first in 1810 in Munich, then capital of Bavaria, the ceremony celebrated a royal wedding for two weeks (Helen Chamber of Commerce 2000). The idea caught on and has been regularly celebrated through the centuries, including drinking traditional thick beer called marzen. In 1970, the first Oktoberfest was held in the re-created village. Although small at first, within five years the fall party became popular and tourists filled the village to capacity. In order to expand the two-week Oktoberfest

Photograph 6.1
Helen, Georgia, "Before"

Courtesy of Alpine Helen/White County Convention and Visitors Bureau, Helen, Georgia.

season, Helen now includes the fall leaf season for a six-week festival period, spanning from mid-September to early November.

Oktoberfest is the major annual event, but Helen has added other events throughout the year to expand its tourist draw. A hot air balloon race, Fourth of July celebration, and concerts attract visitors in the summer months, and art shows and Christmas holiday events pull in tourists during the winter months.

Marketing for the village is provided by the Alpine Helen/White County Convention and Visitors Bureau and is funded primarily through collection of a hotel/motel tax by the village and White County. A Web site provides travel and event information and links to Helen, and there are print materials for mass market mailings. The bureau is a nonprofit entity and is supported by both taxes and private sector businesses.

Outcomes

Helen's story truly represents a best practices application of surrealism for developing a marketing concept. It incorporates all three elements of surrealism approaches—scope, scale, and shock value, or incongruity. The concept has no historical basis, yet the physical setting of the North Georgia Mountains provided a perfect backdrop for the re-creation of an Alpine village. The innovation and willingness of private business owners to take a chance on the concept is testimony to the spirit of the community and the desire not only to survive, but also to thrive as a community. Helen is a case study of how creativity can lead to the total transformation of an economy.

The outcomes are quite impressive: when Helen first embarked on its efforts to re-create itself as an Alpine village, there were six businesses operating in town. Today, there are 200 specialty and import shops and restaurants. Additionally, there are over 1,000 motel or hotel rooms located in Helen and another 1,000 rental cabins, chalets, and cottages in the area. The hotel/motel taxes collected and used for marketing have increased from $180,000 in 1991 to $385,000 in 1999. In 2000, nearly two million visitors traveled to Helen. This represents a remarkable influx of people to a small village of 430 and an incredible transformation from a dying mountain town with no economic prospects to a major tourist destination.

HOLLAND, MICHIGAN
POPULATION: 32,000
CONCEPT: "HOLLAND—YOU DON'T NEED A PASSPORT"

Located on the western shore of Lake Michigan, Holland was founded in 1847. The Reverend Albertus Van Raalte, considered the city's founding father, purchased acreage from the U.S. Government and established a farm on the site. The same family remained in control of the property until it was purchased by the City of Holland in 1983 (Wrona 1995).

The early founders solicited the U.S. Congress for funds to develop a harbor on the shore of Lake Michigan. Efforts to complete the harbor were not successful until nearly fifty years later. By this time, it was too late for Holland to become a viable commercial port, but it was utilized as a harbor to bring in tourists from Chicago. In 1907, a Queen Anne Victorian-style lighthouse was constructed. Decommissioned by the U.S. Coast Guard in 1971, citizens began an effort to save the lighthouse. In 1974, the Holland Harbor Lighthouse Historical Commission was formed and the lighthouse has become a visual asset to the area, known as "Big Red," a beacon of light and historic beauty (Holland Area Convention and Visitors Bureau 1998). Although Holland was noted as a lakeshore resort in the early twentieth century, it was not until the latter part of the century that it became a widely recognized tourist destination. Holland is noted for utilizing the elements of scale and shock value (incongruity) in its application of surrealism.

Selecting the Concept

Holland did not really market itself as a Dutch town until 1929, when a local biology teacher suggested that the city plant tulip bulbs to reflect the town's namesake country. The city now plants and maintains many tulips, with over six million blooming in the springtime (Laukitis 2000). With the planting of the tulips, the community decided to develop a special event, the Tuliptime Festival. Holland pursued the development of the concept and began to add more features that are Dutch in nature. In essence, Holland used its link to the past to form the basis for selecting the concept of a re-created Dutch village.

Developing the Concept

With interest growing in the tulip display each year, the community decided to create the Holland Area Convention and Visitors Bureau in 1988 to further market and manage development of the concept. The goal has been to develop Holland, in conjunction with the city, into an overnight destination (Laukitis 2000:1). Another aspect of the development process has been the willingness of Holland to cooperate with nearby areas, so that attractions can be marketed jointly. The effort to develop the concept is community wide, in that "everyone is considered a partner" (Laukitis 2000:2).

Shortly after the Convention and Visitors Bureau was established, efforts began to identify, purchase, and relocate original historic structures from The Netherlands. The first structure to be brought over and reconstructed is the 250-year old working windmill, the DeZwaan. The remarkable twelve-story-high attraction serves as a point of interest for drawing tourists to Holland (see Photograph 6.3). Tours with costumed guides enhance the experience. The windmill has served as a catalyst for additional development including a gift shop and an authentic Dutch carousel. Dutch Village was developed to re-create a small Dutch town of 100 years ago. The architecture includes bridges, canals, and gardens. A farmhouse, barn, museum, and

Photograph 6.3
The "Famous" Landmark of Holland, Michigan

Courtesy of Holland Area Convention and Visitors Bureau.

specialty stores with items imported from The Netherlands enhance the ambience. Klompen dancers perform in wooden shoes to the music of an Amsterdam street organ at certain times of the year (Holland Area Convention and Visitors Bureau 1999). An authentic wooden shoe factory located nearby completes the effect.

The Van Raalte Farm has been gradually developed to become a unique park for the area. The City of Holland has developed a master plan for the property, focusing on providing re-creational opportunities for citizens and visitors while preserving the historical character of the more than 150-year-old property (Wrona 1995). The property is an intact historic and culturally significant site.

The City of Holland has participated in development of the concept in other ways as well. In 1978, the Downtown Development Authority Board was established to secure "comprehensive public and private support for Downtown revitalization, stressing historic preservation within the context of economic development, and striving towards innovation, and creative ways to plan for Downtown's physical and organizational development" (City of Holland 2001).

In 1984, Holland earned designation as a Main Street community from the National Trust for Historic Preservation's Main Street Program. Several historic properties have been restored or adapted for reuse, and investments in infrastructure improvements have occurred since that time, resulting in an attractive downtown as seen in Photograph 6.4. Projects in progress such as Window on the Waterfront Park and the redevelopment of Windmill Island will enhance the physical attributes of Holland.

The city enacted a special tax, a 2 percent lodging surcharge, in order to fund the Convention and Visitors Bureau. Revenues from this tax average about $350,000 per year, increasing as occupancy rates increase. The bureau uses the funds for operations and marketing programs, including maintaining a Web site as well as publishing numerous printed brochures and other materials.

Both the public and private sector in Holland have joined in the process of creating the concept of a Dutch village. For example, both sectors have actively participated in commissioning and installing statues throughout the area. The Immigrants Statue was sculpted by a well-known artist from The Netherlands and was donated to Holland on its 150th anniversary. The Joy of Music is a group of five statues—three musicians and two singing children, installed by the Lumir Corporation. Private citizens have also donated several statutes.

Outcomes

The Tuliptime Festival alone attracts between 5,000 to 7,500 people each year with its special events and visual attraction of the millions of blooming flowers. The festival is sponsored through ticket, poster, and t-shirt sales, as well as several corporate sponsorships (Laukitis 2000). During the spring, concerts, parades, special cultural events that feature dancing and music, as well as arts and crafts shows are held. Holland has tried, and succeeded, with developing several events so that tourism continues in other times of the year as well. The Dutch WinterFest runs from November 24 until December 17 of each year and features theatre, carriage rides, festive decorations, and other special events such as a parade with reindeer. The Kerstmarkt is held during this time too. This is a traditional European Christmas market, with vendors providing unique gift and food selections in wooden

Photograph 6.4
Historic Downtown, Holland, Michigan

Courtesy of Holland Area Convention and Visitors Bureau.

booths that line the brick pathways of Holland. The Up on the Rooftops tour is held in December to provide a view of historic Holland. On December 1, Sinterklass arrives astride a white horse for an evening of refreshments, caroling, and other festivities. During the fall of each year, several events are held to encourage tourists to visit during the off season. These include a Pumpkin Festival, a festival to cele-brate the migration of Canadian Geese, and various art events, such as a Gallery Walk.

The marketing efforts have paid off for Holland. The average number of visitors per year is approximately three million, with a good distribution of tourists during all seasons. In the early 1990s, much lower hotel occupancy rates were experi-enced in the winter and late fall months. Due to efforts to encourage tourism during all seasons, hotel occupancy in Holland has increased. For example, in 1990 the January occupancy rate was only 34 percent, in 2000, it was 55 percent (Holland Area Convention and Visitors Bureau 2000). Similar gains were made in Febru-ary, November, and December, months that had historically experienced low oc-cupancy rates.

Holland has successfully built upon its Dutch ancestry and created a destination venue for attracting millions of visitors annually. The creativity exhibited in pur-chasing and relocating historic Dutch structures to the City of Holland is extraordi-nary and has served as a basis to enhance the appeal of a re-created Dutch village on the shores of Lake Michigan.

ROSWELL, NEW MEXICO
POPULATION: 49,000
CONCEPT: ROSWELL'S OUT OF THIS WORLD

What exactly happened on June 14, 1947? Roswell has built a concept and helped bolster an economy using this question. That night, rancher W. W. Brazel found strange debris scattered over an area on a sheep ranch northwest of Roswell. The group intelligence officer for the Roswell Army Air Field was alerted and the debris gathered. A press release was issued from the base, with the headline "RAAF Captures Flying Saucer on Ranch in Roswell Region" (Jaroff 1997). After the evidence was shipped to the 8th Air Force in Fort Worth, Texas, another press release was issued stating that the debris was from a weather balloon. Regardless, Roswell's notoriety as a site visited by a UFO has never disappeared, and in recent years has become even more recognized for this event.

It is not so surprising that Roswell would take a chance on mystique as a basis for fostering economic development. Its pioneering spirit is evident from its past: Roswell was founded by a professional gambler in 1870 (Barrett 1996) at the conflu-ence of the Hondo, Pecos, and Spring Rivers. Roswell never became a gaming mecca, but it did grow into a bustling cattle and railroad center (Zendel 1990). The water and surrounding greenery attracted many cattle ranchers and farmers to this town in the Pecos Valley. It is also noted as an area that characters such as Geronimo and Billy the Kid frequented. In the early twentieth century, humorist Will Rogers referred to Roswell as the "prettiest little town in the West" (Kidder 1999:37).

In 1967, the Walker Air Force Base (formerly named the Roswell Army Air Field) was closed. The population of Roswell decreased from 49,000 to 30,000 over the next few years (Zendel 1990). The city took over the property and began actively recruiting businesses to locate in the industrial park crafted from the former base. Roswell successfully attracted several major manufacturers, including a fireworks producer, and a very large mozzarella cheese factory, reputed to be the largest in the United States (Handy 1997). But another major mainstay of the economy has declined over the last several years, the oil and gas industries. In the 1980s, there were between twenty and thirty drilling rigs in the county; as of 1999 there were none (Kidder 1999).

By contrast, the service industries are growing in Roswell, due in large part to the concept marketing approach. As one reporter in a national publication explained, "Roswell has turned Unidentified Flying Object mystique into a nice business" (Barrett 1996:49). Roswell's approach relies heavily on the element of scope: targeting the market intensively.

Selecting the Concept

Roswell has been the subject of speculation regarding the veracity of UFO stories throughout the decades. In 1980, a book entitled *The Roswell Incident* spurred renewed interest in Roswell (Jaroff 1997). Following this, a 1991 report published by the Center for UFO Studies in Chicago charged that a UFO had been recovered in 1947 at the Roswell site and that the government had covered up evidence of it. A sequel, *The Truth About the UFO Crash at Roswell,* in 1994 fed the furor even more (Jaroff 1997:70).

When Thomas Jennings was elected mayor in 1994, it seemed a natural marketing opportunity: the selling of Roswell's mystique. Mayor Jennings, with a degree in marketing, viewed the mystique as another industry that could be developed to help Roswell's economy (Barrett 1996). With declines in manufacturing and in the oil and gas industries, the community decided to try to develop the service economy of Roswell via tourism.

Developing the Concept

The Roswell Chamber of Commerce, the City of Roswell, and other organizations and business leaders joined in the effort to establish the concept marketing approach. Fundraising events were held to cover the costs of marketing materials and activities. Already, interest was growing due to release of publications about Roswell, and also because the International UFO Museum and Research Center opened in 1992. Founded by three retirees who came forward with information about the incident in 1947, the museum began to attract widespread attention. Thus, with the combination of these elements, Roswell had its future in sight and embarked on a public-private partnership to market itself (Walker 2000).

In 1995, a UFO festival was conceived to further promote Roswell's mystique. By the following year, the festival attracted thousands of tourists (Barrett 1996:49). The festival is sponsored by revenues collected from the hotel/motel lodging tax of 6 percent. In 1997 the festivities really took off: a celebration of the fiftieth anniversary of the crash received national media attention. *Time* magazine featured two stories about Roswell that summer, including the cover story for the July 1997 issue. Movie and television performers came to join in the celebration, including cast members from the television series, *Roswell*, and the event generated an estimated $4.5 million of publicity for Roswell (Huckabee 2000). This event helped to further increase recognition of Roswell as a destination, and it became internationally known for its UFO connection. It now attracts visitors not only from the United States, but other countries as well, and is gaining a reputation as an epicenter for UFO research and related activities.

Outcomes

Tourism has increased dramatically since 1992. Visitors are eager to experience Roswell and to seek out venues such as the Crash Café on the television show, *Roswell*, modeled after a real café in town called Aliens' Zone (Walker 2000). Although the television show is not filmed in Roswell, many of the props are produced in town. Another outcome of the media attention has been the filming of several commercials in Roswell.

The city's hotel/motel tax receipts have increased steadily as a direct result of the concept marketing efforts. Table 6.1 summarizes the growth in receipts, reflecting the upward trend from the initial onset of the concept marketing effort, 1994, to the most recent data available, 2000.

Perhaps a more telling analysis is the impact on Roswell's citizens. Per capita personal income has increased from $15,491 in 1994 to $116,614 in 1997, and average hourly earnings in the retail trade sector increased from $7.90 to $8.97 by 1999 (Roswell Chamber of Commerce 2000). Retail and service stores have prospered, with alien memorabilia sold in retail establishments throughout town (Thompson 2000). A variety of items are offered by local artists and entrepreneurs. Another outcome has been the expansion of Impact Confections, a candy company whose products include an alien-shaped lollipop to the once vacant former Levi Strauss factory (Kidder 1999).

Table 6.1
Growth in Lodging Tax Revenues for Roswell

Fiscal Year 1999–2000	$465,157
Fiscal Year 1998–1999	$445,797
Fiscal Year 1997–1998	$431,050
Fiscal Year 1996–1997	$368,017
Fiscal Year 1995–1996	$387,513
Fiscal Year 1994–1995	$349,144

Source: Roswell Chamber of Commerce 2000.

Some citizens would rather not have Roswell marketed on the basis of this mystique. With its name now a "national buzz word connoting both otherworldliness and governmental perfidy," some are uncomfortable with the concept (Handy 1997:62). However, enough citizens support the concept and view it as an industry that can bolster Roswell's economy. This cannot be refuted, as millions of dollars have been garnered by the community through tourism and related activities. Convention and meeting bookings at the Roswell Convention and Civic Center have risen, and five new motels have been built in the period 1998 to 2000 (Thompson 2000). By incorporating the element of scope of a surrealistic concept marketing approach, Roswell has been able to turn its civic distinction of "otherworldliness" into a business.

VALENTINE, NEBRASKA
POPULATION: 3,000
CONCEPT: AMERICA'S HEART CITY

Located on the tableland between the Niobrara and Minnechaduza Rivers, Valentine is positioned within Nebraska's cattle ranching region. The sandy soils do not support much crop raising, but the grasses of the prairie are ideal for grazing cattle. The area offers scenic views, with the backdrop of cliffs along the rivers' edges and the state's tallest waterfall. Famous for its bridges, the area is home to one of the highest railroad bridges in the United States, and the historic cantilevered Bryan Bridge (Valentine Chamber of Commerce 2000). Noted in the past for boisterous outlaws and the famous hide-out just south of town, the Rustler's Roost, not many settlers came to the area until after construction on a fort began in 1880 (Valentine Chamber of Commerce 2000:2). The Sioux City and Pacific Railway Line reached the area in 1883, and in 1884 the village of Valentine was incorporated.

In the 1950s, a dam was built on the Snake River south of Valentine for irrigation purposes. One of the benefits of this major project is that the area attracts thousands of visitors for fishing and other water recreation activities. The Niobrara River is considered to be among the top ten best rivers for canoeing in the United States, and attracts thousands of recreational tourists each year (Valentine Chamber of Commerce 2000:3). Other attractions include the former site of Fort Niobrara that is now a wildlife refuge with buffalo, longhorn cattle, and elk roaming the area. The Cowboy Trial, a biking and hiking trail along the old Sioux City and Pacific line runs right through downtown, attracts numerous visitors each year too.

Now, Valentine is gaining recognition for its Valentine Day activities. The approach Valentine has utilized for developing its concept is based primarily on shock value, or incongruity. The following sections summarize how Valentine transformed from a town known for its cattle ranching to "America's Heart City."

Selecting the Concept

Why Valentine for a name of a small military outpost in ranching territory? Could the settlers envision a future need to associate their town with St. Valentine, the bishop martyred in 270 A.D. who is credited with penning the first valentine card? Actually, the town's name was selected to honor a congressman from Nebraska.

Edward Kimball Valentine served in the U.S. House of Representatives from 1879 to 1871. He gained immense popularity with settlers throughout the region because he was instrumental in passing a bill to protect settlers' interests from unscrupulous land sharks (Valentine Chamber of Commerce 2000). When the town was incorporated in 1884, his name was selected to honor his service to Nebraska's citizens. Thus, Valentine inherited its future basis for a concept marketing approach. At first, it may seem an incongruent concept for a small Nebraska town in ranch country to market itself as a center for Valentine's Day activities. Yet this incongruity adds to its charm, and with the name "Valentine," it stands the test of time.

Developing the Concept

Since the town was named after Congressman Valentine, it seemed logical and natural to use this name to develop a marketing concept. In the United States, Valentine's Day and its traditions had been firmly established by the late 1950s, when the local government, the local schools, and the chamber of commerce decided to gain more recognition as America's Heart City (Jacobs 2001). The basis for their marketing concept was virtually self-selection, given its name.

The community responded with developing several specialty events held each Valentine's Day. Since the Annual Valentine Coronation was already being held each year by the Valentine High School, it seemed logical to expand and build on this basis. Yet, it was not until the idea of remailing valentine cards with the official Valentine seal that the concept became national in scope. Each year, the post office receives thousands of valentine cards from all over the United States and other countries that are remailed with traditional cachet stampings and the official postmark. The postal employees, and Valentine Chamber of Commerce volunteers oversee the processing of between 15,000 and 20,000 cards each year.

The chamber of commerce is also responsible for marketing Valentine and has a budget of nearly $50,000 for these activities (Jacobs 2001). With the advent of the Internet, Valentine has seen a shift in the traditional remailings to include electronic mailings. At its Web site, visitors can select and send electronic postcards from Valentine via e-mail. Additionally, they can choose and purchase a variety of Valentine gifts.

Outcomes

Valentine is an extremely busy town during the month of February. The chamber of commerce sponsors events on Valentine's Day in which couples can be wed by the clerk magistrate of the Cherry County Court. The main focus continues to be the remailing service, and it is that function that has received regional and national attention. Several activities have been implemented that further serve to expand the valentine card mailings each year. For example, a special mailing to many hospitalized veterans in the region was conducted in 2001.

Valentine has developed its community concept marketing approach based literally on what its name implies. Building on the time-honored traditions of Valentine's Day, the community has been able to market itself as America's Heart City, gaining recognition regionally and nationally. While the activities are concentrated in February, marketing helps to gain recognition for the other attractions of Valentine and helps to attract many visitors during other times of the year for recreational activities such as boating, fishing, hiking, canoeing, and bicycling.

SUMMARY

Each community was asked to share advice to others considering developing a concept based on surrealism. The following is a compilation of that advice:

- Plan for the design, placement, and layout of roads from the beginning, as increased traffic will place high demands on infrastructure.
- Plan for parking facilities, including space to accommodate buses and recreational vehicles.
- Work with the public sector to preserve land for public use, rather than just private sector businesses. The ability to offer parks, open space, and other public spaces is important to support the overall concept.
- Try to identify more sources of financial support from the beginning of the concept development.
- Identify the market so that the concept can be tailored to the potential visitors.
- Once the concept is decided upon, stay with it and develop it fully so that it can gain recognition.

Approaches based on surrealism require a high level of creativity in order to be plausible and unusual enough to generate interest. Operating on the principle of creating shock value, surrealistic approaches need to incorporate some element of incongruity. Helen, Georgia, has captured this ability with its re-creation of an Alpine village in the North Georgia mountains. The incongruity of seeing Bavarian village architecture is striking, intriguing, and attractive as evidenced by its continuing popularity through the years. Helen also incorporates the elements of scale as the whole town is an Alpine Village. Valentine, Nebraska, uses incongruity too: Who would expect to find America's Heart City in ranching country that was formerly occupied by outlaws in the nineteenth century? Its name alone has managed to make the concept plausible.

Holland, Michigan, already had the basis of its concept marketing approach based on its history, so it did not have to overcome a high level of incongruity by re-creating itself as a Dutch village. Its creativity, however, places it in the status of surrealism approaches. Purchasing and relocating original historic structures from The Netherlands to their town in Michigan, Holland has managed to add an element of surprise, or the shock value element, that transcends the usual effect of a re-created environment. As with Helen, Holland has implemented the concept on a scale that is large enough to be plausible and attractive. Mount Dora, Florida, has not relocated structures in its efforts to create a New England town atmosphere, but the incongruity of applying an architectural style not of the region qualifies it as a surrealism approach. It literally inherited the concept and has benefited from subsequent marketing of its charm and uniqueness. Mount Dora has also incorporated the element of scale very successfully. The entire town *is* a New England village. Finally, Roswell has captured the attention of many with its ties to UFOs. Building its concept on the question of whether or not the area was really visited by beings from another world, Roswell has successfully integrated this mystique into concept marketing. Roswell's approach and is an excellent example of how to incorporate the element of scope into a surrealism approach: the market is clearly defined and highly targeted.

Surrealistic approaches for building a community marketing concept requires boldness and creativity. It is not for the faint of heart and requires unwavering dedication to make the concept work. A clear indication from the case studies presented in this chapter is that the development of the concept requires a strong commitment to the idea, and that it may take some time to fully implement all the elements needed to become a destination based on the concept.

7

Pulling It All Together: Ideas and Implications for Communities

The process of identifying, designing, and implementing a community concept marketing approach is complex and multifaceted, and requires a high level of energy, dedication, and resources. Few communities have the level of resources needed to rely solely on marketing techniques such as those used by the private sector. Success requires integration of the concept marketing approach with comprehensive community development planning and action.

Development implies change. Preferably, the changes will be desirable community outcomes. Development plans must be evaluated in terms of the changes that will impact all facets of the community including social, economic, physical, political, and environmental dimensions, and all should be considered to achieve balance (Laws 1995). The responses to change typically taking the following forms:

1. Watch it (passive response).
2. Wait until it is a crisis and then respond (reactive response).
3. Plan for it (proactive or anticipatory response).

The third approach enables communities to anticipate and prepare for change, rather than react to it.

Community concept marketing calls for something else too: the creation of a vision. As Forman and Mooney (1999:12) explain:

Every community needs a vision if it wants to go somewhere and be able to know when it has arrived. A vision will: guide the organization to its intended goal, remind the community what it represents, inspire the people who take pride in their community, control those unrelated activities, [and] free the community of past failures.

The vision serves as a guiding force for the community and is absolutely necessary in order to accomplish effective community economic development.

Community concept marketing can be effectively designed and implemented using a variety of strategies as illustrated in the previous chapters. Most of the concept marketing approaches integrate tourism as a major component in the development strategy. Tourism can have dramatic impacts on a community, and the evaluation must consider the scope and magnitude of these impacts. Some degree of tension is inevitable as tourism-based development strategies imply social and environmental changes (Pearce, Moscardo, and Ross 1996). So care must be taken not to alienate the community.

ASSESSING APPLICABILITY

Capitalizing on underutilized resources to generate growth and development has served as the guiding principle for this book. Sometimes the assets or resources are not obvious; other times, they are readily apparent. This leads to the first step in assessing the applicability of a concept marketing approach in a community: an audit of resources. Some refer to these resources as cultural capital, or what makes a community unique (Kearns and Philo 1993:ix).

Community assessments, or audits, are often used in economic development planning. In the context of creating a concept marketing approach, the community audit considers all the resources of an area, not just those related to physical infrastructure or labor force characteristics. For example, it would include a survey of citizens' skills. Do special skills exist in the community, such as traditional craftsmanship or unique musical talents?

Community audits also includes a review of available or potential financial resources. Are public funds available? Is the private sector willing to invest in the concept? Is there a possibility of public-private sector collaboration? There is another important aspect of the resource audit that goes beyond financing: Are there leadership resources in the community? What organization could facilitate the process? Is there enough interest and commitment from the civic and private sectors to make the concept happen?

The next step in the process is more complex, as it requires not only the initial development of the concept, but also a comprehensive evaluation of potential effects on and integration with the community's overall goals. Based on the resource audit and gauging of community interest, the initial concept marketing idea should be identified at this stage. Is it an identifiable theme or concept? What is the market appeal, and how segmented is the appeal? Does the community have the resources to implement the plan? What are the alternatives and the benefits and costs of the concept marketing idea?

Further, the concept must be designed with community development in mind. Several techniques can be utilized, including citizen participation venues to assess community receptivity to the concept and to identify desired goals and outcomes. Will it be acceptable to a majority of citizens? Will there be positive outcomes?

What negative outcomes could occur? How will it impact the physical, social, economic, political, and environmental aspects of the community? Some of the communities profiled conducted a process such as this, which guided the implementation of the concept marketing approach. Others stated that in retrospect, they wish they had evaluated the concept more comprehensively from the outset, to avoid unanticipated negative outcomes.

Once the concept is identified and integrated with overall community plans, and the initial market is assessed, a comprehensive marketing plan should be designed. Public and nonprofit organizations must be willing to fully research the potential market and design the approach accordingly. This can be an expensive component of the process, although some state departments of economic development help communities prepare and gather marketing information. Several of the communities profiled lamented the fact that they did not have a marketing plan when they started and that outcomes would have been easier with the information gained from designing a comprehensive marketing plan.

Following the marketing plan, communities develop an implementation plan. Which organization(s) will be responsible for various aspects of implementation? Who will pay for it? Is it a collaborative effort? Will there be special taxes levied or other means to finance the concept's implementation? What is the timeframe for implementation? Implementation requires integration of the overall community development plan with appropriate funding.

The final component of the process is evaluation. Too often, community economic development organizations fail to properly evaluate their actions. Without evaluation, it is difficult to adjust the concept plans and activities to achieve maximum benefits. Evaluation also provides the opportunity to gauge whether or not the community's desired goals and outcomes are being achieved. If so, the concept marketing approach can be considered successful. After all, it is the community that wants the satisfaction of achieving desired outcomes. If problems arise and negative outcomes are generated, evaluation helps the community discover the underlying causes and adjust the approach. Either way, evaluation is essential. The concept marketing approach should have periodic evaluations built into it.

IMPLICATIONS

Communities have to make decisions about how they use limited resources. Concept marketing approaches are risky. For every success story, there are numerous stories of failed attempts. Many communities in which concepts were applied most successfully had few other development options. In some, their isolated location would not attract industrial or other revenue-generating activities. Others were faced with the demise of their communities unless the economics changed. In these cases, the concept marketing approach was the development strategy of last choice. Perhaps this pressure provided the catalyst that spurred positive change and desirable economic development outcomes.

Virtually every community profiled in this book experienced some sort of negative outcome as a result of implementing concept marketing approaches. These tended to be related to the physical environment, such as increased traffic congestion or property price increases that outpaced the buying power of the citizenry. Many of these communities have been forced into a reactive posture, responding to issues as they arise. Others have anticipated these outcomes by integrating the concept approach carefully with the community's overall development plans, by implementing zoning and other land use regulations to guide growth.

Because the concept marketing approach holds the potential to dramatically change the community, the stakes are high. As with any high-stakes endeavor, the politics have to be considered. At this point, it is crucial for the community to keep in mind the goals of the concept marketing approach. Focusing on the goals inspires the community to find the time, energy, and other resources that are required to make concept marketing a success.

Bibliography

Adler, Jerry. "Theme Cities." *Newsweek* 126, no.11 (September 11, 1995): 68–70.

Albers, Jan. *Hands on the Land*. Rutland, Vermont: Orton Family Foundation, 2000.

Alpine Helen/White County Convention and Visitors Bureau. "2000 Travel Guide." Helen, Georgia, 2000.

The American City & County. "Tourism Leads to Water and Wastewater Upgrades." *The American City & County* 113, no. 4 (April 1998): 16–17.

American Economic Development Council. *Economic Development Today: A Report to the Profession*. Schiller Park, Illinois: AEDC, 1984.

Amusement Business. "Something for Everybody at Hersheypark." *Amusement Business* 109, no. 32 (1997): 17–20.

Applegate, Jane. "For Iowa Town, Bestseller Provides a Bridge to Prosperity." *The Washington Post*, December 6, 1993, p. F10.

Arvidson, Sandra L. "Loveland: A Niche in the Arts." *Colorado Business Magazine* 16, no. 3 (March 1989): 28–32.

Ashworth, G. J., and H. Voogd. *Selling the City: Marketing Approaches in Public Sector Urban Planning*. London: Belhaven Press, 1990.

Association for the Preservation of Historic Natchitoches. "Melrose, A National Historic Landmark." Natchitoches, Louisiana: Association for the Preservation of Historic Natchitoches, 2000.

Austin Convention & Visitors Bureau, "SPAM Musuem." Austin, Minnesota: Austin Convention and Visitors Bureau, 2001.

———. www.autincvb.com/attractions/html, November 7, 2000.

Baar, Aaron. "It's No Margaritaville." *Adweek* 20, no. 11 (March 16, 1998): 3.

Bailey, Elizabeth. Letter and information to the author, April 19, 2000.

Barrett, William P. "Unidentified Flying Dollars." *Forbes* 158, no. 2 (July 15, 1996): 49–51.

Bartlette, Delani. Letter and information to the author, April 21, 2000.

Beare, Nikki. Telephone interview and information to the author, November 21, 2000.

Beinecke, Walter. Personal interview, June 29, 2001.

Benini, Carla. "The Sweet-Smelling Heart of the Hershey Empire." *Meetings & Conventions* 29, no. 6 (May 1994): 110–115.

Berryman, Anne. "Film Projects Add $17.6 million to Economy." *Georgia Trend* 14, no. 2 (October 1998): 88.

Beyard, Michael D., Ray Braun, Herb McLaughlin, Patrick L. Phillips, and Michael Rubin, et al. *Developing Urban Entertainment Centers*. Washington, D.C.: Urban Land Institute, 1998.

Bingham, Richard D., and Robert Mier, eds. *Theories of Local Economic Development*. Newbury Park, California: Sage Publications, 1993.

Blakely, Edward J. *Planning Local Economic Development*. Thousand Oaks, California: Sage Publications, 1994.

Boaz Chamber of Commerce. www.boaz.al.us/history/history.html, 2001.

Boling, F. Wayne. "Pursuing the Factory Outlet Development." *Economic Development Review* 13, no. 2 (1995): 89–90.

Brack, Elliott. "Two Mountain Towns Thriving on Bavarian Theme." *Atlanta Constitution* (June 3, 1994): p. 2, col 1.

Brammer, Rick, and Jack Tomasik. "Retail Potential Analysis for Local Economic Development." *Economic Development Review* 13, no. 2 (1995): 32–42.

Brannon, Jody. "Thanks to 'Exposure,' Tiny Roslyn Is a Star." *Variety* 347, no. 5 (May 18, 1992): 61–64.

Brooks-Pittman, Edna. Telephone interview, May 1, 2000.

Burgett, Jackie. Telephone interview, April 21, 2000.

Burke, Edmund M. *Corporate Community Relations: The Principles of the Neighbor of Choice*. Westport, Connecticut: Quorum Books, 1999.

Butcher, Lola. "From Larry King to NY Times, Branson Is Hot Topic." *The Kansas City Business* 10, no. 32 (April 24, 1992): 8.

Cain, Steve. "Boom in Boaz." *American Demographics* 12, no.1 (January 1990): 56–58.

Calamba, Sheila. "The Toast of This Wisconsin Town May Be a Beer Stein Big as the Ritz." *Wall Street Journal,* 12, no. 1 (June 25, 1996): Sec. B., p.1.

Cane River National Heritage Commission. "Cane River Creole." Natchitoches, Louisiana: Cane River National Heritage Commission, 2000a.

———. "Cane River National Heritage Area." Natchitoches, Louisiana: Cane River National Heritage Commission, 2000b.

Cape May County Planning Board. "Population Estimates and Projections, 1970–2020." Cape May, New Jersey: Planning Board, 2000.

Casazza, John A. *Shopping Center Development Center*. Washington, D.C.: Urban Land Institute, 1985.

Castells, Manuel. *The Informational City, Information Technology, Economic Restructuring, and the Urban-Regional Process*. Oxford: Blackwell, 1989.

Cermak, Adam. Telephone interview, May 16, 2001.

Chase, Henry. "Old Times Not Forgotten: Natchitoches and the Cane River Country." *American Visions* 10, no. 1 (1995): S6–10.

Clark, Kim. "Chocolate Pilgrims Find Paradise in Pennsylvania." *U.S. News & World Report* 128, no. 16 (April 24, 2000): 72.

City of Branson. "Branson Profile." Branson, Missouri: City of Branson, 2000.

City of Canton. www.cityofcanton.net/com/canton/movies.htm, November 7, 2000.

City of Eunice. "Visitor's Guide to Eunice, Louisiana's Prairie Capital." Eunice, Louisiana: City of Eunice, 2001.

———. "Eunice Historic District Commission." Eunice, Louisiana: City of Eunice, 2000.

City of Holland. "About Mainstreet and the Downtown Development Authority." Holland, Michigan, 2001.

City of Loveland. www.ci.loveland.co.us/rialto/rialto.htm, November 4, 2000.

City of Mount Dora. "Historic Preservation in the City of Mount Dora." Mount Dora, Florida, 1997.

City of Mountain View. "City and County Sales Tax, 1999 and 1998." Mountain View, Arkansas, 2000.

City of Solvang. "Sales Tax and Bed Tax Receipts." Solvang, California: City of Solvang, 2000.

City of Toppenish. "Toppenish Guide." Toppenish, Washington: Community Development, 2000.

City of Vacaville. www.vacavillevip.com/business.htm, December 20, 2000.

Clarke, Susan E., and Gary L. Gaile. *The Work of Cities*. Minneapolis: University of Minnesota Press, 1998.

Coffey, Gary. "Celebrating 90 Years at the Corner of Cocoa and Chocolate." *Amusement Business* 109, no. 32 (August 11, 1997): 15–19.

Coleman, Calmetta. "Making Malls (Gasp!) Convenient." *Wall Street Journal*, February 8, 2000, p. B1.

Coolidge, Shelley Donald. "On-Site Filmaking: A Boon to States' Coffers, Cameras Roll for 'The Crucible' after Massachusetts Goes to Unusual Heights to Outbid Other Locations." *Christain Science Monitor*, September 25, 1995, p. 1.

Constantino, Fred. Telephone interview, November 13, 2000.

Convention and Visitors Bureau of Fredericksburg Texas. "The Arts in Fredericksburg, Texas and the Texas Hill Country." http://www.fredericksburg-texas.com/arts/index.htm, 2000.

Conzen, Michael P., ed. *The Making of the American Landscape*. Boston, Massachusetts: Unwin Hyman, 1990.

Corbett, Jennifer. "The King of Canned Meat Gets the Last Laugh." *Los Angeles Times*, July 6, 1995, p. A5.

Couch, Jan. "The Fertile Triangle: Fort Collins, Greeley and Loveland Blossom into Dynamic Communities." *ColoradoBiz* 26, no. 11 (November 1999): 59–65.

Coy, Peter. "Land of Milk and Armani." *Business Week* 3352 (December 27, 1993): 3032.

Crawford, Margaret. "The World in a Shopping Mall." In *Variations on a Theme Park: The New American City and the End of Public Space*, Michael Sorkin, ed. New York: Hill and Wang, 1992.

Crilley, Darrel. "Architecture as Advertising: Constructing the Image of Redevelopment." In *Selling Places: The City as Cultural Capital, Past and Present*, Gerry Kearns and Chris Philo, eds. New York: Pergamon Press, 1993.

Curtis, Wayne. "Belle Epoxy." *Preservation*, 52, no. 3 (May/June 2000): 32–39.

Daily, Laura. "Made in America." *Geico Direct* (Fall 2000): 2.

Davis, Mae. "Festival of Antiques Revitalizes City." *Nation's Cities Weekly* 20, no. 8 (May 19, 1997): 8.

DeCaro, Frank. "Looking for an Outlet." *New York Times Magazine*, April 6, 1997, pp. 70–74.

Di Salvatore. "City Slickers." *New Yorker* 69, no. 5 (March 22, 1993): 40–49.

Dickinson, Mike. "Corning: Crystal City of the Finger Lakes." *Conservationist* 51, no. 1 (August 1996): 17–18.

Dorsey, Jennifer. "In Madison County, Iowa, a Popular Novel Brings Visitors." *Travel Weekly* 52, no. 75 (September 23, 1993): 12.

Downtown Business Association. www.downtownvacville.com/community/htm, Vacaville, California, October 20, 2000.

The Economist. "Movie Tourism in America's Mid-West." *The Economist* (October 30, 1999): 20.

The Economist. "Utopia, Missouri." *The Economist* 333 (December 24, 1994): 25–28.

The Economist. "The Sewers of Madison County." *The Economist* 336 (September 23, 1995): 220.

Egan, Timothy. "Old-Fashioned Town Sours on Candymaker's New Pitch." *New York Times*, October 6, 1997, p. A1.

Ettorre, Barbara. "Charity Begins at Home." *Management Review* 84, no. 2 (1995): 4–36.

Eureka Springs Chamber of Commerce. "Tourism in a Nutshell." Eureka Springs, Arkansas, 1996.

Eureka Springs Historical Museum. "The Eureka Springs Historical Museum." Eureka Springs, Arkansas, 2000.

Eureka Springs Parks and Recreation Commission. "The Springs and Parks of Eureka Springs." Eureka Springs, Arkansas, 2000.

File, Karen Maru, and Russ Alan Prince. "Cause-Related Marketing and Corporate Philanthropy in the Privately Held Business." *Journal of Business Ethics* 17, no. 14 (1998): 1529–1539.

Fiscus, Chris. "A Steppingstone to Hollywood: Tucson Emerges as TV, Film Haven." *Arizona Business Gazette*, May 17, 1991, p. 1.

FitzSimmons, Jill. "Legends Casino Run Gambling Gamut." *Tribune Business News,* May 12, 1998.

Fletcher, Jeff. "Deliberately, San Marcos' Economy Grows." *Nation's Cities Weekly* 16, no. 27 (July 5, 1993): 1–2.

Flint Publishing, Inc. "Discover the Yakima Valley." Toppenish, Washington, 2000.

Florida Department of Revenue. Information to the author, December 18, 2000.

Florida Planning. "In the Public Eye." May 1999, pp. 3, 8.

Forman, Maury and Jim Mooney. *Learning to Lead, A Primer on Economic Development Strategies.* Dubuque, Iowa: Kendall Hunt Publishing Company, 1999.

Forstner, Sandy. Telephone interview, December 15, 2000.

Fox, Larry. "The Out of Towners: Hershey, Pennsylvania." *The Washington Post*, August 27, 1999, p. 32.

Fox, Richard L. "Mount Dora: A Century-Old Florida Town Evokes New England Charm." *Where to Retire* (spring 2000): 10–14.

Fredericksburg Chamber of Commerce. "History and Economy." http://www.fredericks burgtexas.net/coc.htm, 2000.

Friends of Roslyn. www.moosefest.com/perm-pages/rba.htm, June 4, 2001.

Garner, Karen. Letter and information to the author, December 15, 2000.

George A. Hormel & Co. *The Hormel Legacy: 100 Years of Quality.* Austin, Minnesota, 1991.

Gill, Ronnie. "Corning, N.Y.: The Sparkling Crystal City." *New York Times*, April 18, 1999, p. E5.

Gillespie, Angus. "Folk Festival and Festival Folk in Twentieth-Century America." In *Time Out of Time: Essays on the Festival*, Alessandro Falassi, ed. Albuquerque: University of New Mexico Press, 1987.

Gillespie County Historical Society and Commission. "Gillespie County Historical Society History." http://www.pioneermuseum.com/gchshist.htm, 2000.

————. "Gillespie County and Fredericksburg, Texas." Fredericksburg, Texas: Fredericksburg Chamber of Commerce, 1981.

Gingerich, Amy. "Vacaville's Vacancies Vanish." *The Reporter*, Vacaville, California, December 16, 2000.

Gold, John R., and Stephen V. Ward, eds. *Place Promotion: The Use of Publicity and Marketing to Sell Towns and Regions*. New York: John Wiley & Sons, 1994.

Golden, Daniel. "Mr. Hershey's Wishes? The Question Hinders His Super-Rich School." *The Wall Street Journal*, August 12, 1999, pp. A1, A6.

Goodey, Brian. "Art-Full Places: Public Art to Sell Public Spaces?" In *Place Promotion, The Use of Publicity and Marketing to Sell Towns and Regions,* John R. Gold and Stephen V. Ward, eds. Chichester, New York: John Wiley & Sons, 1994.

Gottdiener, Mark. *The Theming of America, Dreams, Visions, and Commercial Spaces.* Boulder, Colorado: Westview Press, 1997.

Groff, Bernard, and Diane Weiland. Telephone interview, April 19, 2000.

Gruen, Nina. "What You Should Know and What You Can Do About the Revolutionary Changes in Retailing." *Western City* (May 1994): 5–6.

Hageman, William. "Artificial Snow Turns Town into a Winter Wonderland." *The Times-Union,* Jacksonville, Florida, December 10, 2000, p. D6.

Hall, Colin Michael. *Tourism and Politics: Policy, Power and Place.* New York: John Wiley & Sons, 1994.

Hall, Colin Michael, and John M. Jenkins. *Tourism and Public Policy.* London: Routledge, 1995.

Hamilton, Teresa. "Factory Stores at Nut Tree Key to Finances of Growing Vacaville." *The Business Journal Serving Greater Sacramento.* 10, no. 8 (May 17 1993): 17–19.

Handy, Bruce. "Roswell or Bust: A Town Discovers Manna Crashing from Heaven and Becomes the Capital of America's Alien Nation." *Time* 149, no. 25 (June 23, 1997): 62–68.

Harper, Iris. Telephone interview, September 1, 2000.

Harris, Mary. Telephone interview, May 15, 2001.

Harrisburg-Hershey-Carlisle-Perry Co. Tourism & Convention Bureau. "2000 Visitors Guide." Harrisburg, Pennsylvania: The Barash Group, 2000.

Harvey, David. *The Condition of Postmodernity.* Oxford, England: Basil Blackwell, 1989.

Hattes, Ann. "These Southern Living History Festivals, Events and Attractions Will Send You." *AAA Southern Traveler* (July/August 1999): 22–24.

Heath, Ernie, and Geoffrey Wall. *Marketing Tourism Destinations: A Strategic Planning Approach.* New York: John Wiley & Sons, Inc., 1992.

Heitman, Vicky. Telephone interview, May 15, 2001.

Helen Chamber of Commerce. http://ngeorgia.com/travel/oktoberfest.html, August 23, 2000.

Hemphill, Thomas A. "Corporate Governance, Strategic Philanthropy, and Public Policy." *Business Horizons* 42, no. 3 (1999): 57–62.

Henderson, Keith. Telephone interview, October 27, 2000.

Hershey Foods Corporation. www.hersheypa.com/history/milton_history.html, November 11, 2000.

Heubusch, Kevin. "Jobs at Play and Jobs that Pay." *American Demographics* 20, no. 5 (May 1998): 50–56.

Himmelstein, Jerome L. *Looking Good and Doing Good: Corporate Philanthropy and Corporate Power.* Bloomington, Indiana: Indiana University Press, 1998.

Hirschman, Albert O. *The Strategy of Economic Development.* New Haven: Yale University Press, 1958.

Hoelscher, Steven D. *Heritage on Stage: The Invention of Ethnic Place in America's Little Switzerland.* Madison: The University of Wisconsin Press, 1998.

Hoke, Linda. "The Impact of the Arts on Economic Development." *Southern Growth Update* 21, no. 4 (Summer 1996): 1.

Holland Area Convention and Visitors Bureau. "2000 Occupancy Analysis." Holland, Michigan: April 2000.

———. "Attractions." Holland, Michigan: 1999.

———. "Big Red, Holland's Historic Lighthouse." Holland, Michigan: 1998.

Hollinger, Hy. "Big Bucks Ride on Race to Host Film Crews." *Variety* 340, no. 7 (August 22, 1990): 69–71.

Hornaday, Ann. "If You Film It There, the Tourists Will Surely Come." *The New York Times,* August 14, 1994, Sec. 2, p.16.

Howland, Marie. "Applying Theory to Practice in Rural Economics." In *Theories of Local Economic Development,* Richard K. Bingham and Robert Mier, eds. Newbury Park, California: 1993.

Huckabee, Dusty. Telephone interview, May 3, 2000.

Hull, Sandra. Telephone interview, September 6, 2000.

———. "Partnership on Main Street." National Main Street Center (May/June 1994): 2.

Iowa Department of Economic Development. "The Economic Impact of Travel on Iowa Counties." Des Moines, Iowa: Division of Tourism, 2000.

Jacobs, Dean. Telephone interview, May 18, 2001.

Jaffe, David. *Levels of Socio-Economic Development Theory.* London: Praeger, 1998.

Jaroff, Leon. "Did Aliens Really Land? An Examination of Events in 1947 Shows Something Did Happen. But the Resulting Stories Got Out of Hand and Out of This World." *Time* 149, no. 25 (June 23, 1997): 68–72.

Johnson, Jan Thomas, and Grace Broughton. "1996 Great American Main Street Awards." *Main Street News* 122 (May/June 1996): 3–4.

Johnson, Kelly. "Galleria Outpaces Other Big New U.S. Malls in Leasing." *Sacramento Business Journal* 17, no. 13 (July 7, 2000): 13.

Kammlah, Joe. Telephone interview, September 11, 2000.

Kauffman, Ben. "Stand-In for Cicely." *Philadelphia Inquirer,* October 4, 1992, Sec. R, p. 6.

Kearns, Gerry, and Chris Philo, eds. *Selling Places: The City as Cultural Capital, Past and Present.* New York: Pergamon Press, 1993.

Keese, Susan. "Rebirth in Bellows Falls." *Vermont Life Magazine* (Summer 2000): 35–37, 81.

Kelley, Tina. "Caveat Emptor: Can't Fight City Hall? Don't Try to Buy It." *Christian Science Monitor,* October 27, 1997, p. 15.

Kerby, Roberta. Telephone interview, May 1, 2000.

Kidder, Lyn. "More than UFOs." *New Mexico Business Journal* 23, no. 5 (June–July 1999): 3739.

King, Thomas. "In Which Our Reporter Ponders What Hollywood Did to Iowa, and Vice Versa." *The Wall Street Journal*, July 27, 1995, p. B1.

Koch, Kathy. "The New Corporate Philanthropy." *The CQ Researcher* 8, no. 8 (1998): 169–192.

Kosminsky, Jay. "Venture Philanthropy, A New Model for Corporate Giving." *Fund Raising Management* 28, no. 6 (1997): 28–31.

Kotler, Philip, Donald Haider, and Irving Rein. "There's No Place Like Our Place! The Marketing of Cities, Regions, and Nations." *Public Management* 76, no. 2 (February 1994): 15–18.

Krohn, Lee. Letter and information to the author, May 21, 2001.

———. Telephone interview, October 27, 2000.

Kunstler, James Howard. *Home From Nowhere*. New York: Touchstone, 1996.

Lackey, Susan A., and Charles Eckenstahler. "The Forgotten Role of Retail in Economic Development." *Economic Development Review* 13, no. 2 (1995): 85–87.

Laukitis, Sally Hallan. Telephone interview, May 2, 2000.

Laws, Eric. *Tourism Destination Management, Issues, Analysis and Policies*. London: Routledge, 1995.

Levy, John M. *Contemporary Urban Planning*. Upper Saddle River, New Jersey: Prentice-Hall, 1997.

Lockwood, Bill. "Bellows Falls Gets Downtown Designation." *Town Crier* 39, no. 41 (February 25, 2000): 1.

The Longaberger Company. "The Story Behind the Basket." Newark, Ohio: 2000.

Loveland Chamber of Commerce. "Loveland Relocation & Visitors Guide." Fort Collins, Colorado: The Northern Colorado Business Report, 2000.

Loveland Sculpture Group. http://lovelandsculpturegroup.org, January 25, 2001.

Loveland Visitors Center. www.loveland.org/arts_main.htm, November 4, 2000.

Lukas, Paul. "270 North Dakotans Branded by Corporation! The Ultimate Company Town." *Fortune* 139, no. 3 (February 15, 1999): 48.

Lyons, Thomas S., and Roger E. Hamlin. *Creating an Economic Development Action Plan*. Westport, Connecticut: Praeger Publishers, 2001.

Main Street Program. National Trust for Historic Preservation. www.mainst.org, March 15, 2001a.

———. National Trust for Historic Preservation. www.mainst.org, March 29, 2001b.

Main Street Wooster, Inc. "Main Street Viewpoint." Wooster, Ohio, 1995.

Malizia, Emil E., and Edward J. Feser. *Understanding Local Economic Development*. New Brunswick, New Jersey: Center for Urban Policy Research, 1999.

Maltbie, Wanda. Telephone interview, November 2, 2000.

Mannix, Margaret. "Nashville's Comeback Try." *U.S. News & World Report* 117, no. 1 (July 4, 1994): 64–69.

Marcel, Joyce. "A Town's Artful Revival." *Boston Globe*, April 16, 2000, p. B9.

Marks, John. "Riding Out of the Sunset: Why the Comeback Kid of the 1990's Is the One and Only John Wayne." *U.S. News & World Report* 119, no. 20 (November 20, 1995): 14–16.

Marx, Jerry D. "Corporate Strategic Philanthropy: Implications for Social Work." *Social Work* 43, no. 1 (1998): 34–41.

McCall, Mary Ann. Telephone interview, September 8, 2000.

McGarry, T. W. "Party Seeks to Draw Hollywood to Wisconsin." *Los Angeles Times*, September 15, 1997, p. B3.

McKaughan, Molly. "Is Corporate Philanthropy Drying Up?" *Across the Board* 32, no. 4 (1995): 21–26.

McManus, Sue. Telephone interview, November 17, 2000.

Medrano, Maricela. Telephone interview, March 15, 2000.

Merriam-Webster Inc. *Webster's Ninth New Collegiate Dictionary.* Springfield, Massachusetts: Merriam-Webster Inc., 1988.

Meyers, Carleton R. "Attracting Factory Outlet Stores Can Spell Success for a Community." *Economic Development Review* 13, no. 2 (1995): 51–55.

Moen, Judy. Telephone interview, May 23, 2001.

Moody, Ginny. Telephone interview, May 1, 2000.

Morgan, Rita. Telephone interview, September 18, 2000.

Mount Dora Area Chamber of Commerce. "Mount Dora Florida." Heron Publishing: Spring Hill, Florida, 2000.

———. "History of Mount Dora." Mount Dora Area Chamber of Commerce: Mount Dora, Florida, 1999.

Murphy, Brian. "Volunteerism: Another Kind of Giving." *Across the Board* 32, no. 4 (1995): 25.

Natchitoches Area Chamber of Commerce. "Natchitoches Christmas Season." Natchitoches, Louisiana, 2000.

Natchitoches Convention and Visitors Bureau. "Natchitoches Parish, Louisiana Fairs and Festivals, 2001." Natchitoches, Louisiana, 2000.

Natchitoches Parish Tourist Commission. "Hotel/Motel Occupancy Tax Report." Natchitoches, Louisiana, 2000a.

———. "Cane River Country." http:www.Natchitoches.net/tourism/caneriver_natchitoches. htm, 2000b.

Nation's Cities Weekly. "Branson, Missouri, Offers Big-Time Fun and Small-Town Hospitality." *Nation's Cities Weekly* 23, no. 18 (May 8, 2000): 8.

National Conference of State Legislators. *Economic Impact of the Arts.* Washington, D.C., 1987.

National Main Street Center. *Main Street,* no. 12 (May/June, 1996).

Nelson, Rex. "Eureka's Year-Round Appeal." *Arkansas Business,* November 4, 1991.

Nelson, Richard R. *The Sources of Economic Growth.* Cambridge, Massachusetts: Harvard University Press, 1996.

New Glarus Chamber of Commerce. "History of New Glarus Wisconsin." http://www.new glaruswi.com/html/history.html, 2000.

New Glarus Historical Society. "Swiss Historical Village." New Glarus, Wisconsin, 2000.

Newark & Licking County Chamber of Commerce. "Newark's History." Newark, Ohio: 2000.

———. "Licking County Community Profile." Newark, Ohio: 1997.

Noble, Gary. Telephone interview, June 7, 2001.

Nykiel, Ronald A., and Elizabeth Jascolt. *Marketing Your City, U.S.A: A Guide to Developing a Strategic Tourism Marketing Plan.* New York: The Haworth Hospitality Press, 1998.

O'Mara, W. Paul, Michael D. Beyard, and Douglas M. Casey. *Developing Power Centers.* Washington, D.C.: Urban Land Institute, 1996.

Organization for Economic Co-operation and Developent (OECD). *Creativity, Innovation and Job Creation.* Paris, 1997.

Palombo, Mike. Telephone interview, November 3, 2000.

Patterson, Kim. Letter and information to the author, April 20, 2000.

Pearce, Jennifer. Information sent to the author, March 15, 2000.

Pearce, Philip L, Gianna Moscardo, and Glenn F. Ross. *Tourism Community Relationships*. Oxford: Pergamon Press, 1996.

Pegler, Martin M. *Retail Entertainment*. New York: Visual Reference Publications, 1998.

Phillips, Patrick D. "Merging Entertainment and Retailing." *Economic Development Review* 13, no. 2 (1995): 13–15.

Phillips, Rhonda. "Using Corporate Strategic Philanthropy for Economic Development." *Economic Development Review* 17, no. 1 (August 2000a): 7–11.

———. "What Are the Positive Impacts of Retail-Based Economic Growth for Communities?" *Journal of Shopping Center Research* 7, no. 1 (spring/summer 2000b): 7–28.

———. *Art as a Small Business Development Approach: Exploring the Feasibility of an Arts Business Development Program for Hattiesburg, Mississippi*. University of Florida: Center for Building Better Communities, December 1998.

Philo, Chris, and Gerry Kearns. "Culture, History, Capital: A Critical Introduction to the Selling of Places." In *Selling Places: The City as Cultural Capital, Past and Present*, Gerry Kearns and Chris Philo, eds. New York: Pergamon Press, 1993.

Pittman, Robert, and Rhonda Phillips. "When Does Retail Count as Economic Development?" *Economic Development Review* 13, no. 2 (1995): 4–6.

Powell, Tom. "Hershey Stadium Earns Another No. 1 Ranking." *Amusement Business* 108, no. 57 (December 16, 1996): 45–47.

Quintanilla, Carl. "Planning a Vacation? Give Some Thought to Spamtown USA." *Wall Street Journal,* April 30, 1998, pp. B1, B18.

———. "A Seven-Story Basket Goes Up in the Fields of Ohio." *Wall Street Journal*, October 15, 1997, pp. B1, B18.

Ranney, Eldon. Telephone interview, January 19, 2001.

Ransom, Ed. Telephone interview, December 18, 2000.

Reder, Alan. "The Wide World of Corporate Philanthropy." *Business and Society Review* 92 (1995): 36–42.

Richards, Bill. "Ririe, Idaho, Has Stars in Its Eyes about a Space Station." *Wall Street Journal,* October 16, 1996, Sec. A, p. 1.

Ricks, Ingrid. "To Tour Alaska, Head East on I-90." *The Seattle Times,* May 27, 1993, East Life Section, p. 2.

Riddle, Marcy. Information to the author, November 2, 2000.

Rife, Joanne. *Solvang, Denmark in the USA*. Solvang, California: Book Loft, 1978.

Rockingham Arts and Museum Project. "Art Makes a Difference." Bellows Falls, Vermont: RAMP, 2000a.

———. "*Art2*." no.1 (spring 2000b): 1.

Roman, Monica. "Godzilla Ignites Production Surge." *Variety* 3688 (September 29, 1997): S7–9.

Roswell Chamber of Commerce. "Economic Development Report." Roswell, New Mexico, May 2000.

Rovero, Dan. Telephone interview, November 4, 2000.

Royal, Weld. "Citizenship Starts at Home: Corning Inc. Rebuilds Its Upstate New York Community and Plans for Global Charity." *Industry Week* 249, no. 13 (August 21, 2000): 83–86.

Rush, Van. "The Rackensack Folklore Society." *Arkansas Democrat*, June 14, 1964, p. B2.

Rypkema, Donavan D. *The Economics of Historic Preservation, A Community Leader's Guide.* Washington, D.C.: National Trust for Historic Preservation, 1994.

Sagawa, Shirley, Eli Segal, and Rosabeth Moss Kanter. *Common Interest, Common Good: Creating Value Through Business and Social Sector Partnerships.* Cambridge, Massachusetts: Harvard Business School Press, 1999.

Samuels, Cindy. Telephone interview, May 15, 2001.

Schiesser, Elda. Telephone interview, September 6, 2000.

Schmidt, Kathleen. "Promotions of Place." *Marketing News* 33, no. 19 (September 13, 1999): 9–10.

Schwanke, Dean, Terry Jill Lasseter, and Michael Beyard. *Remaking the Shopping Center.* Washington, D.C.: Urban Land Institute, 1994.

Seel, Irene. Letter and information to the author, May 2, 2000.

Shipley, Tonya. "A Year Later, 'Popeye' Still Missed." *Advocate* 179, no. 87 (March 17, 2000): A1.

Shipman, Jane. Letter and information to the author, April 28, 2000a.

———. Telephone interview, April 21, 2000b.

Smith, Charles. Mayor, Town of Boaz, Alabama. Interview, March, 2000.

Smith, Craig. "The New Corporate Philanthropy." *Harvard Business Review* 72, no. 3 (1994): 105–117.

Smith, Robert. "A Success Story: Bellows Falls Praised for Revitalization." *Eagle Times,* May 18, 2000, pp. B1, B3.

Somaya, Shilph. "Non-Philanthropic Corporate Involvement in Community Development." *Business and Society Review* 97 (1996): 32–38.

Solvang California Conference and Visitors Bureau. "Destination Guide 2000." Solvang, California, 2000.

Sorkin, Michael, ed. *Variations on a Theme Park, The New American City and the End of Public Space.* New York: Hill and Wang, 1992.

Spectrum Publications. "Wooster Community Guide 2000." Orrville, Ohio: 2000.

Springfield Missouri Chamber of Commerce. www.springfieldmo.org/generalinfo/, October 20, 2000.

Stocker-McLane, Elizabeth. "New Glarus Celebrates its 150th." *SwissBusiness,* no. 2 (March–April 1995): 54–56.

Stone County Leader. "Visitors Guide." Mountain View, Arkansas, 2000.

Strand, Debbie. Telephone interview, May 23, 2001.

Sullivan, Joanna. "Jodi Foster Set to Bring Movie." *Baltimore Business Journal* 12, no. 26 (November 18, 1994): 2–3.

Szymanski, Jim. "Movie Complex Developers Race to Build in Auburn, Washington." *The News Tribune,* Tacoma, Washington, March 20, 1996, p. B1.

Thompson, Leslie. Telephone interview, May 1, 2000.

Town of Havana. www.historichavana.com/townhall.townhall_p2.htm, November 2000.

Traylor, Jackie. Telephone interview, September 18, 2000.

Tritt, Donald G. *Swiss Festivals in North America.* Morgantown, Pennsylvannia: Mashof Press, 1999.

U.S. Department of Interior, National Park Service. "National Register of Historic Places, Inventory-Nomination Form, Eureka Springs Survey, Carroll County, Arkansas." October 1, 1980.

———. "National Register of Historic Places, Inventory-Nomination Form, Cape May, New Jersey." Form 10-300a, December 14, 1970.

Vacaville Chamber of Commerce. www.vacavillechamber.com/history.htm, October 20, 2000.

Valentine Chamber of Commerce. www.valentine-ne.com/history/history.htm, November 11, 2000.

Vermont Arts Council. "Historic Exner Block Opens Its Doors to Artists." *Artsletter*, no. 3 (Fall 2000): p. 9.

Vermont Forum on Sprawl. *Growing Smarter, Best Site Practices for Residential, Commercial & Industrial Development*. Burlington, Vermont: 2001.

Wagner, Dina. Telephone interview, June 7, 2001.

Walden, Barbara. Letter to the author, November 6, 2000.

Walker, Charlie. Telephone interview, May 3, 2000.

Walkup, Carolyn. "Restaurateurs Sing Sad Tune about Branson: Overdevelopment Sparks Competition." *Nation's Restaurant News* (June 12, 1995): 2.

Walnut Area Development Association. Www.showcase.netins.net/web/walnutiowa/business.htm, January 20, 2001.

———. "Manifest of Opportunities." Walnut, Iowa: 1999.

Walnut Merchants Association. http://showcase.netms.net/web/walnut/walnuthistory.htm, 2001.

Walter, Bob. "Roseville, California Retail Project Awaits Tentative Agreements." *The Sacramento Bee*, February 13, 1997, p. 213B.

Ward, Stephen V. *Selling Places: The Marketing and Promotion of Towns and Cities, 1850–2000*. New York: Routledge, 1998.

Weeden, Curtis. "How Much *Should* a Company Give?" *Across the Board* 32, no. 4 (April 1995): 22–23.

White, Cheri. "The Springs of Eureka: Still Magic After All These Years." *The Flashlight Visitor's Guide*, Eureka Springs, Arkansas, 1998.

Willis, Craig. Telephone interview, May 18, 2001.

Winchell, Dick G. "Northern Overexposure." *Planning* 58, no. 1 (January 1992): 24–26.

Witt, Christy Parks. "Havana's Historic Walking Tour Guide." *The Havana Merchant* 3, no. 2 (October–December 2000): 1, 5.

Wolcott, John. "Can Auburn Cope with Gargantuan Retail?" *Puget Sound Business Journal* 14, no. 52 (May 13 1994): 18.

Wolf, Michael J. *The Entertainment Economy: How Mega-Media Forces Are Transforming Our Lives*. New York: Times Books, 1999.

Wooster Area Chamber of Commerce. www.wooster-wayne.com/chamberdemographics.htm, August 23, 2000.

Wrona, Mark. "City Cultivates Historic Farmstead for Park." *Public Works* 126, no. 7 (June 1995): 62–64.

Ybor City Development Corporation. "Ybor City Update and Development Summary." Ybor City, Florida, March 2000.

Ybor.org. "Tampa's Historic Landmark District." 2000.

Yellin, Emily. "Grisham Script Troubles Town in Mississippi." *New York Times*, November 19, 1995, p. A19.

Zendel, Denise. "Roswell, New Mexico." *New Mexico Business Journal* 14, no. 10 (October 1990): 57–70.

Zuckerman, Michael. Telephone interview, April 21, 2000.

————. "The Mid-Atlantic Center for the Arts and Rebirth of Cape May, 1970–1997." In *Cape May, Queen of the Seaside Resorts, Its History and Architecture*. Cape May, New Jersey, September 1998.

Index

About the Author

RHONDA PHILLIPS is Director of the Center for Building Better Communities and an Assistant Professor in the Urban and Regional Planning Department at the University of Florida.